CUSTOMER ADOPTION
REIMAGINED

STRATEGIES TO WIN EARLY ADOPTERS AND
DRIVE MARKET SUCCESS

BERKLEY A. BAKER

Copyright © 2025 by Berkley A. Baker. All rights reserved.

All rights reserved. No part of this book may be reproduced or transmitted in any form or by any means, electronic or mechanical, including photocopying and recording, or by any information storage and retrieval system, without the prior written permission of the author.

Limit of Liability/Disclaimer of Warranty: The author has made every effort to ensure the accuracy and completeness of this book but makes no guarantees or warranties, express or implied, regarding its content. This includes but is not limited to, warranties of merchantability or fitness for a particular purpose. No warranty is extended through sales representatives or written materials. The advice and strategies provided may not be applicable to your specific circumstances, and professional consultation is recommended where appropriate. Neither the author nor the publisher shall be held liable for any losses, including but not limited to profits, commercial damages, or incidental or consequential damages.

eBook ISBN 978-1-7344832-1-5

Trade Paperback ISBN 978-1-7344832-3-9

Illustrations and cover design: Jenée Baker

DEDICATION

To my wife, Jenée. Your unwavering love, encouragement, and belief in me have been my greatest source of strength.

To Josiah, Amanda, and Amarie. You inspire me every day with your dreams, your determination, and the incredible people you are becoming.

ACKNOWLEDGMENTS

This book is the result of the collective wisdom, support, and collaboration of many remarkable individuals and organizations who've shaped my journey.

Mom, thank you for instilling in me a love of learning and the belief that education can transform lives. And dad, thank you for encouraging me to attend West Point and for your steady support ever since.

To my colleagues in the medical device industry, hospital executives, physicians, and nurses. Your insights have shaped my understanding of how innovative solutions can drive customer adoption and improve patient care.

A heartfelt thank you to the entrepreneurs and startup founders who have taught me about courage, adaptability, and resilience. Your stories of navigating uncertainty and overcoming challenges have inspired me daily.

To my collaborators at the Advanced Technology Development Center, your commitment to fostering entrepreneurial growth has had a lasting impact. The team at the Russell Innovation Center for Entrepreneurs has been equally inspiring in its dedication to innovation, showing me what's possible when creativity and purpose intersect.

To the students, alumni, mentors, and colleagues from Georgia State, Georgia Tech, Emory, Morehouse, ASEBUSS, West Point, and beyond. Thank you for the invaluable opportunities to grow, collaborate, and make meaningful contributions. Your curiosity, insights, and shared experiences have challenged me to think differently, constantly refining my approach to entrepreneurship and leadership.

Finally, to the countless individuals and organizations striving to bring innovation to life, this book is for you. Your resilience, determination, and belief in change are the true drivers of progress.

Special thanks to Gerald, Jennifer, David, Charles, Nate, Florin, Recha, Malcolm, Julie, Jane, Joey, John, Jay, A.T., Dana, Obi, Anthony, Bi Li, Sandy, Scott, MT, Louise, Matt, Barry, Mark, Mike D., Pete, Marty, Tiffany, Eleanor, Rodney, Megan, Randy, Alex, and many others. Each of you has been part of this incredible journey.

This book would not have been possible without you.

TABLE OF CONTENTS

ACKNOWLEDGMENTS 4

CHAPTER 01
THE ADOPTION CRUCIBLE 9
The Need for a New Path. 20
Overview of this Book 25

CHAPTER 02
RETHINKING ADOPTION 29
A Framework for Innovation Adoption 34

CHAPTER 03
INTRODUCTION TO CFOSS® CUSTOMER ARCHETYPES .53
Core Customer: Problem Pioneers 54
Financial Customer: Fiscal Architects. 63
Operational Customer: Productivity Gurus 70
Strategic Customer: Visionary Trailblazers 77
Social Customer: Network Ambassadors 82
Navigating Customer Complexities 88

CHAPTER 04
UNVEILING THE LAYERS OF CFOSS® VALUE 93
Core Value Propositions: The Foundation of Value Creation . . 96
Maximizing Financial Value: Unlocking Economic Benefits. . 100
Enhancing Operational Value: Optimizing Efficiency 104
Harnessing Strategic Value: Gaining Competitive Advantage . 110
Fostering Social Value: Building Community. 115
Orchestrating Holistic Value 120

CHAPTER 05
THE HAZARDS OF MISMATCHING 127
Avoiding CFOSS Mismatches: A Proactive Approach 131
Aligning CFOSS Propositions for Success 134

CHAPTER 06
MASTERING YOUR CFOSS® SYMPHONY 139
Unlocking the Broader Potential of CFOSS 164
Conclusion: The CFOSS Journey Beyond the Start Line 166

AFTERWORD 170

APPENDIX A: LESSONS FROM ROBOTIC SURGERY
(CFOSS® CUSTOMERS).............................172
APPENDIX B: LESSONS FROM ROBOTIC SURGERY
(CFOSS® VALUE PROPOSITIONS) 181
APPENDIX C: CFOSS® ARCHETYPE VALUE MATRIX ...189
APPENDIX D: LESSONS FROM ROBOTIC SURGERY
(CFOSS® MISMATCHES) 194
    CFOSS Mismatches................................194
    Exploring the Consequences of Mismatches..............196
    Addressing Mismatches: Solutions and Adjustments 196
ENDNOTES.. 200

Scan to watch the Chapter Overview Video.
Get a quick summary, key insights, and what to look for in the upcoming chapter.

CHAPTER 01

We don't see things as they are, we see them as we are.
–Anaïs Nin

The Adoption Crucible

In the early days of rolling out robotic surgery programs, every interaction felt like walking a tightrope. My role wasn't merely to advocate for the technology. It was to navigate the deep skepticism of a room full of stakeholders and convince them that this innovation wasn't just the future of surgery but a tangible tool that could transform patient care.

The promise of robotic surgery was immense: minimally invasive procedures with unparalleled precision, faster recovery times, and fewer complications. Yet turning that promise into practice was anything but straightforward. The operating room, sterile, bright, and steeped in tradition, was a crucible where innovation met resistance at every turn.

I remember the first time I watched a surgeon sit at the console of a robotic system during a training session. With no patient involved, the physician guided the robotic arms with focused curiosity, testing the system's responsiveness and precision. "This feels more like a video game than surgery," he remarked with a wry smile, intrigued but cautious. For seasoned surgeons, whose expertise was honed through years of practice, the robotic system represented an evolutionary tool that promised to enhance their capabilities. My role wasn't only to sell the mechanics of the system but to show how it could seamlessly integrate into their workflow, preserving the artistry of their craft while pushing its boundaries.

But surgeons were only the first hurdle. Hospital administrators, the ultimate decision-makers, were an entirely different challenge. The financial stakes were daunting. Robotic systems weren't just another equipment purchase. They were multimillion-dollar investments that had to compete with other critical hospital initiatives such as new facilities, expanded service lines, infrastructure upgrades, etc. Every dollar allocated to robotics was a dollar not spent elsewhere, making the rationale even more difficult. Maintenance contracts, disposable instruments, and potential upgrades made the price tag a growing concern for budget-conscious administrators. I sat through countless boardroom meetings armed with clinical studies, cost analyses, and market data, yet every conversation seemed to come back to a single question: "How do we know this will pay off?"

One particular moment stands out. After a two-hour presentation outlining the clinical benefits and strategic advantages of robotic surgery, the CFO of a major metropolitan hospital leaned back in her chair and said, "This all sounds impressive, but how do I explain to our board spending millions on a system that might sit idle?" Her words underscored the fragility of early adoption, where skepticism and uncertainty could stall even the most compelling innovations.

And then there were the patients. While some were captivated by cutting edge technology, others approached it with caution. The word *robot* conjured images of cold, impersonal machines, and their fears needed to be addressed with care. I understood their hesitation on a personal level. My father, my mother, my father-in-law, and even my wife all underwent robotic-assisted procedures. Before each surgery, I found myself having the same conversation, not as a professional advocating for the technology, but as a son, a husband, and a concerned family member.

"Your surgeon will always be in control," I would explain. "The robot isn't replacing them. It's enhancing their skill, allowing for greater precision and better outcomes." Even with all my experience in the field, I wasn't immune to the anxiety that comes with a loved one going under the knife. But I also knew the life-changing potential of this technology. Bridging the gap between patient apprehension and understanding wasn't simply part of my job. It was personal. I had seen firsthand how these conversations could transform fear into confidence, as they had for countless patients and their families.

Yet, even when everyone was aligned, operational challenges loomed large. Robotic systems demanded a reimagining of hospital workflows. Some operating rooms had to be retrofitted, surgical teams trained, and procedures adapted to account for new complexities. I worked alongside nurse managers and operating room coordinators to integrate the technology into daily practice, but progress was often slow and fraught with resistance. The systems were complicated, the learning curves steep, and the stakes were high.

One hospital's experience crystallized the challenges we faced. They had invested heavily in robotic systems, but for months, the machine gathered dust in a storage room.[1] The surgeons weren't ready, the staff wasn't trained, and the administrators were losing patience. It took weeks of building trust, live demonstrations, and personalized support to get the program off the ground. But when it did, the transformation was remarkable. Recovery times plummeted, patient satisfaction soared, and the hospital became a regional leader in robotic surgery. It was a triumph, but one that came at the end of a long and arduous road.

As I reflect on those experiences, I realize that the story of robotic surgery isn't unique. Industries across the board encounter the same friction when groundbreaking ideas meet deeply entrenched norms. Tesla, for example, faced a similar struggle in its effort to revolutionize transportation with electric vehicles, overcoming not only technical barriers but also societal perceptions.

Tesla's Journey

In the mid-2000s, Tesla wasn't the powerhouse it is today but a scrappy upstart fighting to make electric vehicles viable. The idea of an electric car wasn't new, but many still saw them as slow, impractical, and unappealing.

Tesla sought to change that narrative with the Roadster, a sleek sports car that promised high performance and zero emissions. Early adopters faced major hurdles including limited charging infrastructure, a high price tag, and skepticism about reliability. Elon Musk and his team didn't just market the Roadster; they built a community around it, engaging customers who were passionate about sustainability and innovation.

More than a product, Tesla positioned itself as a catalyst for change in transportation and beyond. They addressed operational concerns by building charging networks, appealed to financially conscious customers by emphasizing long-term cost savings, and positioned Tesla as a sustainability pioneer. These efforts turned skeptics into advocates, setting the stage for mass-market models like the Model Y and Model 3.

Still the journey was anything but smooth. Tesla faced production delays, funding crises, and public scrutiny. Traditional automakers dismissed electric vehicles as a niche market. But Tesla persevered, proving that aligning innovation with customer priorities is key to overcoming adoption barriers. Today, Tesla's dominance in the automotive industry proves that even revolutionary ideas must be nurtured to thrive.

The challenge of driving adoption, whether for electric vehicles, robotic surgery, or any disruptive idea, goes beyond the product itself. It's about shifting mindsets, overcoming skepticism, and creating a movement that compels people to embrace change.

This struggle isn't limited to technology. Some of the most profound adoption trials exist in the realm of social change, where resistance is rooted in deeply held beliefs. No one understood this better than Dr. Martin Luther King Jr.

How does your innovation challenge existing norms or perceptions?

Redefining Social Innovation

Dr. Martin Luther King Jr. was an innovator in social change. His approach of nonviolent resistance was a radical strategy that depended on mass adoption to succeed. But convincing people to embrace it wasn't easy.

Many activists, frustrated by years of oppression, questioned nonviolence. Others feared backlash. But Dr. King knew that for real change to occur, his movement needed to capture the moral high ground and win the support of skeptics and moderates.

To religious leaders, he spoke in the language of morality. To young activists, he offered the strength of unity. To politicians, he framed equality as the essence of democracy. He also navigated operational challenges, organizing large-scale marches and boycotts and addressing financial constraints through grassroots fundraising.

The Montgomery Bus Boycott was a masterclass in adoption strategy. While it was rooted in the resolve of the Black community, many of whom relied on buses for their livelihoods, it succeeded through a broader coalition of coordinated action and sustained commitment.

Dr. King connected the immediate goal of desegregation to a larger pursuit of justice, giving people a reason to persevere through adversity. By aligning the boycott with both the immediate goal of desegregating buses and the broader vision of equality, Dr. King inspired people to endure hardship for a greater cause.

Dr. King's legacy shows that social innovation, like technological innovation, requires more than a bold idea. It demands stakeholder understanding and alignment with their priorities. His ability to turn skepticism into belief and division into unity remains a model for driving meaningful change.

The Adoption Crucible and CFOSS®

These stories show that while innovation is exhilarating, but adoption is often an uphill battle. The journey from concept to acceptance hinges not only on the brilliance of an idea, but on the ability to navigate the messy, complex gap between vision and reality. Whether addressing a surgeon's hesitation, a consumer's skepticism, or a community's resistance, adoption is as much about psychology and trust as it is about technology or strategy.

The robotic surgeon, the early Tesla driver, and the Montgomery Bus Boycott participants all faced doubt and resistance. But their stories reinforce an essential lesson. Adoption happens when innovation aligns with what matters most to people.

The Adoption Stalemate

Over the years, working with hundreds of entrepreneurs. Whether as the healthtech catalyst at the Advanced Technology Development Center (ATDC) or the execute lead catalyst at the Russell Innovation Center for Entrepreneurs. I've seen the same challenge play out time and time again. A founder has an idea, often a brilliant one. They secure early validation, maybe even land a few promising pilots. There's momentum, excitement, and a sense that they are on the verge of something transformative. And then, suddenly, everything slows. Traction stalls. The initial enthusiasm fades. It's not a colossal failure, but it's not success either.

This is what I call the adoption stalemate. A cycle where growth hinges on resources, yet resources remain out of reach without growth.

Figure 1.1: The adoption stalemate illustrates common barriers that hinder market adoption of new products or innovations.

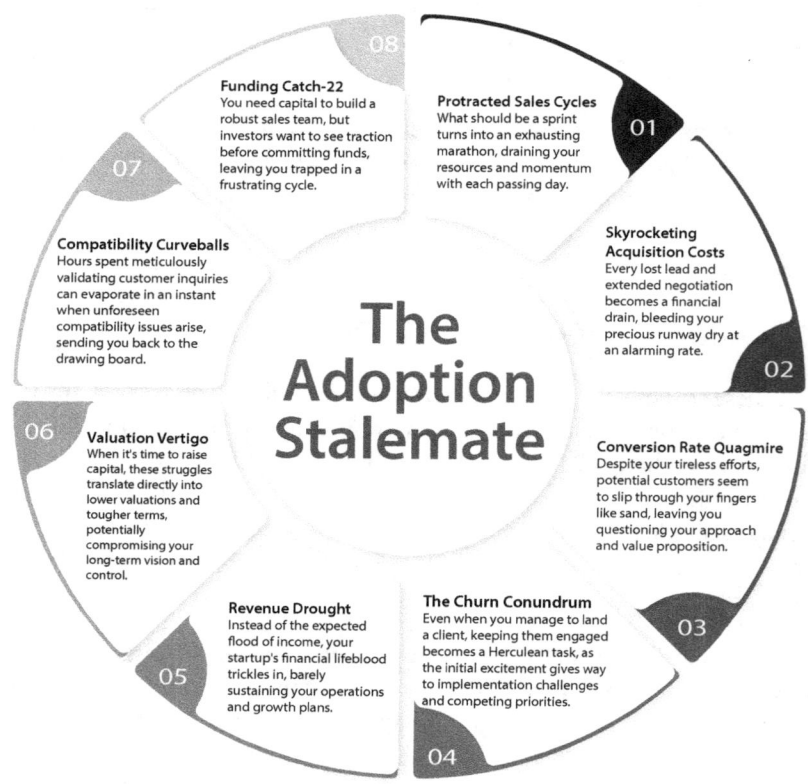

I saw this firsthand with a company developing real-time customer feedback technology. Their product allowed businesses to capture instant customer sentiment through simple, on-site feedback devices, giving organizations a live pulse on customer satisfaction. The value proposition was clear: actionable insights, improved service, and higher retention. Early adopters loved the tool, using it to adjust staff responsiveness and enhance customer experiences.

But larger enterprises, the ones that could scale adoption, were hesitant. They had existing customer feedback systems and layers of internal decision-making. Executives wanted proof in the form of sustained improvements in customer satisfaction, peer validation, and financial performance. Yet, without major enterprise clients, the company couldn't generate the large-scale case studies decision-makers demanded. They were stuck.

This challenge isn't unique to startups. Corporate innovators face the same barriers. Even within large organizations, promising initiatives often require early results to justify continued investment. Without clear traction, projects struggle to secure internal buy-in, resources shift elsewhere, and what once seemed like a game-changing innovation is quietly shelved.

The same cycle played out in a corporate setting with an AI-driven knowledge-sharing tool. The pilot showed promise, but when it came time to expand, the initiative stalled. Department leaders questioned its effectiveness, compliance teams raised governance concerns, and executives wanted clear productivity gains before committing resources.

The adoption stalemate stems not only from financial barriers but from a lack of momentum. Founders burn through their runway waiting for traction that never materializes. Corporate innovators see promising initiatives deprioritized until they fade away.

Breaking free requires more than persistence. It demands a shift in thinking. Adoption isn't about proving an innovation works. It's about aligning with what matters most to customers. Without that alignment, even the most transformative ideas struggle to gain traction.

Have you ever hit a wall when trying to drive adoption? What impact did that stall have on your organizational goals or outcomes?

The Pitfalls of Convention

It's crucial to understand why conventional wisdom often leads innovators astray. Familiar frameworks, comforting as they may be, can act like a siren song. They draw young companies toward strategies that don't align with the realities of early-stage adoption. The result? Wasted time, resources, and momentum.

Let's unpack three common pitfalls that derail startups and prevent innovations from gaining traction.

1. The Technology Adoption Life Cycle (TALC) Trap

Some adoption tests are easy to anticipate. Others reveal themselves only when an innovator assumes customers will behave in predictable ways. TALC provides a seemingly logical road map, but true adoption rarely follows a straight path.[2] Stories of adoption in practice help illustrate where this model falls short.

Static Categories Ignore Fluid Behavior

TALC categorizes customers based on their adoption tendencies, but these tendencies aren't fixed. A company that eagerly embraces one innovation may be hesitant about another, depending on the perceived value, risk, and strategic alignment. Adoption behavior is fluid. An early adopter in one context might act as a late majority in another.

Figure 1.2: The innovation adoption curve illustrates the distribution of market segments and their proportion within the total market, highlighting how different groups adopt new products or innovations over time.[3]

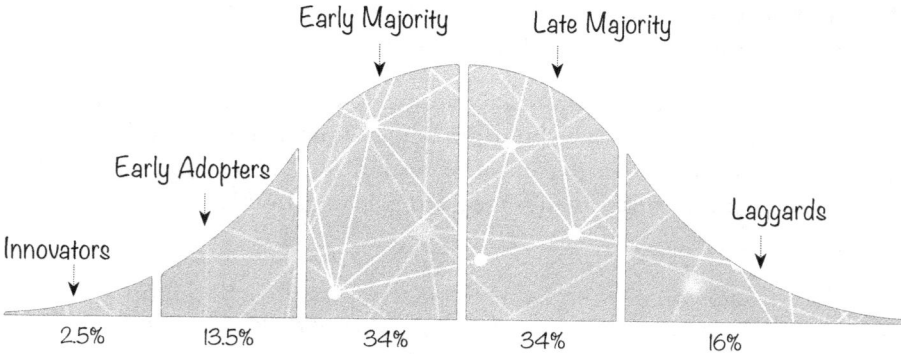

Consider the adoption of telemedicine. A large health system with cutting-edge technology might still hesitate to adopt virtual care, citing physician resistance, workflow concerns, or reimbursement uncertainty. Meanwhile a small rural clinic, traditionally perceived as a technology laggard, might aggressively implement telemedicine because it directly addresses patient access concerns. This highlights a critical flaw in rigid adoption models. Customers don't have permanent personas.

The Nonadopter Blind Spot

TALC assumes that all customers will eventually adopt an innovation. It's just a matter of when. Laggards may take longer, but the framework suggests they'll get there in time. But not all customers are laggards. Some are true nonadopters. As long as they have alternatives, they will never convert. Traditional models fail to account for this, leaving innovators blind to a critical reality. Some potential customers are simply never going to buy in, no matter how much time passes.

Take cashless payments. Many businesses have gradually shifted away from cash, yet some will never go fully digital. Local vendors in rural markets, privacy-conscious consumers, and businesses catering to unbanked populations often reject cashless not because they're late to adopt, but because it fundamentally doesn't align with their needs. A payments company that labels them as slow adopters may waste time and resources trying to convert them, when it should instead focus on refining its approach for those more open to adoption. Understanding why someone won't adopt can be as valuable as understanding why someone will.

Tech Tunnel Vision

TALC is often associated with technology adoption, but adoption challenges extend far beyond tech. A company improving customer service through better training, rather than new software, faces resistance just as real. Employees hesitate, managers demand proof, and executives need return on investment (ROI). Because no new technology is involved, these hurdles are often overlooked in TALC-driven conversations. The issue isn't that TALC can't apply, but we tend not to apply it outside of traditional tech contexts.

This bias overlooks how adoption dynamics shape movements, policies, and new ways of working. The civil rights movement, for example, wasn't about technology, but Dr. King's philosophy of nonviolent resistance still required buy-in, overcoming skepticism, and shifting entrenched behaviors. Adoption involves more than technological progress. It requires getting people to embrace new ways of thinking and operating. Innovators who recognize this can apply adoption strategies more effectively, whether they're launching software, services, or social change.

2. The Funding-First Trap

Venture capital can seem like the golden ticket to success, but the relentless pursuit of funding often leads startups astray. I've seen too many founders believe that raising capital will solve their adoption challenges only to realize they've built their business on untested assumptions.

Here's the trap:

» Startups that prioritize fundraising over customer validation risk making promises they can't deliver. They build perfect pitch decks, but their actual customers remain hypothetical, never engaged, and never tested.

» Instead of using funding to better understand and meet customer needs, startups may find themselves chasing priorities that emerge too early, before they've figured out what their customers actually want.

The most successful founders flip this script. They gather data by immersing themselves in customer realities. They ask probing questions, challenge their own assumptions, and refine their product in ways that make scaling more intentional.

3. The Perils of Indiscriminate Pursuit

If the TALC trap leads innovators to misunderstand adoption behavior and the funding-first trap causes them to chase investors before customers, this next pitfall emerges when founders focus on customer acquisition but in all the wrong ways.

The Consequences of Chasing Everyone

In the race to gain traction, many startups fall into the trap of chasing every potential customer regardless of fit. This scattershot approach spreads resources thin, weakens messaging, and ultimately slows down adoption.

The consequences:

» **Wasted Effort:** A startup that tries to appeal to everyone ends up resonating with no one. When an early-stage company targets vastly different customer groups at the same time, product development and sales efforts become fragmented.

» **Brand Dilution:** Constantly adjusting messaging to fit different audiences weakens a company's identity. When you lack clarity on who your core customer is, it's difficult to build strong advocacy and word-of-mouth momentum.

» **Missed Opportunities:** In chasing any customer who might buy, startups often overlook those who would truly value and champion their product. The best early customers aren't just buyers, they're evangelists who create ripple effects in the market.

The turning point comes when startups focus on their best-fit customers. The ones who not only need their solution but are ready to adopt it. Tesla, for example, didn't start by selling to the mass market. They focused on a niche audience of wealthy car buyers who valued performance and sustainability, then expanded to broader segments.

The lesson? Depth is often more valuable than breadth in early adoption. Finding the right first customers can make all the difference between struggling for traction and building unstoppable momentum.

Understanding these pitfalls isn't merely an academic exercise. It serves as a wake-up call. TALC assumes customers follow a predictable journey, but adoption is messy and nonlinear. The funding-first trap shows how chasing investors before validating customers may lead to fragile foundations. And the indiscriminate pursuit of customers drains resources and stalls momentum rather than accelerating it.

If these conventional strategies so often fail, what should innovators rely on instead?

Rather than rigid models that assume one-size-fits-all adoption patterns, innovators need adaptable frameworks that help them navigate uncertainty and align their strategies with the diverse realities of customer behavior.

Have you relied on traditional adoption models like TALC in your business? If so, where have you found them helpful, and where have they fallen short?

The Need for a New Path

Imagine trying to navigate an unfamiliar city without a map, let alone a GPS. You might stumble across landmarks and make some progress, but you'd waste time retracing your steps, hitting dead ends, and struggling to find the clearest path forward. The journey of innovation adoption often feels the same, filled with potential yet plagued by uncertainty. Traditional models like TALC offer rough road maps, but they often fail to capture the real-life complexities of customer adoption.

As a sales leader in the medical device industry, I worked with a variety of healthcare innovations that faced these obstacles. Today, working with startups in incubators and accelerators, I continue to see entrepreneurs confronting similar hurdles as they try to bring their innovations to market and gain widespread adoption. They have great products and compelling value propositions, but their adoption slows or stops. Not because their solutions aren't valuable, but because they aren't aligning with the factors that truly drive customer decisions. I kept coming back to my own experiences in the field, comparing the successes and failures I had witnessed firsthand, and I realized something critical. Adoption involves more than the technology or the problem being solved. It depends on how well the innovation aligns with the priorities of the customers evaluating it.

The Role of Frameworks

The realization that adoption depends on alignment, not simply innovation, led me to rethink how we navigate the complexities of customer decision-making. It wasn't enough to identify a problem or build a solution. Innovators needed a way to translate those insights into strategies that resonated with their audience. That's where frameworks come in.

Frameworks are not rigid instructions. They're tools that bring structure to the chaos of adoption. Similar to the instruments in an airplane cockpit, they help you navigate through turbulence, guiding decisions and keeping you focused on what matters most.

Of course, no framework is perfect. As the statistician George Box famously said, "All models are wrong, but some are useful." The best frameworks aren't rigid blueprints. They're adaptable tools that evolve with the realities of each unique innovation journey. The promise of frameworks is not perfection, but progress.

CFOSS: The Foundation of Customer Adoption

In the unpredictable landscape of innovation adoption, clarity is power. Recognizing these limitations, I developed CFOSS to offer a more comprehensive, adaptable approach to innovation adoption. CFOSS is built on five interconnected pillars: Core, Financial, Operational, Strategic, and Social. The framework serves not only as a model for understanding adoption but as a practical tool for aligning innovations with the priorities of customers and stakeholders.

CFOSS emerged from both research and experience. During my doctoral work, I wanted to understand why robotic surgery adoption moved faster than other medical innovations, despite its complexity. Later, working with entrepreneurs and corporate leaders, I saw the connection between adoption and alignment with customer priorities. CFOSS reveals patterns behind why some innovations succeed and others don't.

At its heart, CFOSS is a multi-dimensional approach to adoption. Unlike traditional models that focus on a single factor like cost or functionality, CFOSS captures the full spectrum of motivations that drive customer decisions. The five pillars are:

» **Core:** The essential need or challenge the innovation addresses.
» **Financial:** The economic performance, including ROI and cost considerations.
» **Operational:** How the innovation affects existing systems, workflows, and processes.
» **Strategic:** The long-term advantages that strengthen market position and differentiation.
» **Social:** The effect on communities and key stakeholder groups.

But CFOSS doesn't simply map these dimensions. It interconnects them, reflecting the reality that customer decisions are rarely one-dimensional. A hospital administrator may see robotic surgery as a financial decision, but their surgeons view it through operational and strategic lenses, while patients prioritize social and core considerations. Successful adoption requires speaking to all of these perspectives.

The power of CFOSS lies in its adaptability. Whether you're introducing a revolutionary medical device, a software platform, a social initiative, or even a consumer good, the framework scales to meet the demands of your innovation and the complexity of your market. Customer adoption comes from crafting strategies that engage the right audiences, inspire action, and drive sustainable growth. It depends on navigating the complex interplay of customer priorities, economic viability, operational feasibility, strategic positioning, and societal outcomes. The innovations that endure are the ones that strike the right balance across these dimensions.

Figure 1.3: The five interconnected pillars of the CFOSS framework that drive innovation adoption.

The Innovation Adoption Pathway: Bringing CFOSS to Life

Understanding CFOSS is only the beginning. Putting it into action is what drives adoption. The IAP provides a structured, five-step approach to move from concept to adoption.

Step 1: Define the Innovation
» Clarify the specific innovation before assessing customer response.

Step 2: Tuning into Your Audience
» Identify core, financial, operational, strategic, and social customer behaviors for the innovation.

Step 3: Composing the Value Propositions
» Tailor value propositions to resonate with each CFOSS archetype.

Step 4: Harmonizing Value and Needs
» Align value propositions with each archetype's needs to build trust and drive adoption.

Step 5: Fine-Tuning for Success
» Responding to feedback and market signals.

Why CFOSS Matters

The IAP brings CFOSS to life, creating alignment between innovations and customer concerns. CFOSS is a GPS for innovators navigating the complexities of customer adoption. CFOSS serves as a guide, providing focus and clarity to help you move forward with purpose and sidestep common pitfalls.

What sets CFOSS apart is its ability to address customer needs from multiple angles. By prioritizing the opportunities that matter most, CFOSS keeps innovators from spreading themselves too thin, instead focusing efforts where they'll have the greatest impact. Most importantly, CFOSS turns adoption perils into a strategic advantage. It empowers organizations to gain momentum and align their innovations with what truly matters to customers. The table below highlights how CFOSS differs from conventional adoption models like the TALC.

A Comparative Perspective: Traditional Models vs. CFOSS

Aspect	Conventional Adoption Models (e.g., TALC)	CFOSS Approach
Customer Focus	Segments customers into fixed categories	Identifies dynamic customer archetypes
Adoption Drivers	Assumes adoption is driven primarily by product features and market timing	Focuses on aligning value propositions with the specific priorities of different customer groups
Barriers to Adoption	Assumes resistance stems from lack of awareness or understanding of product's value	Recognizes resistance as multifaceted, often stemming from mismatches between value propositions and customer archetypes
Customer Engagement	Treats customer personas as fixed, assuming a customer who was an early adopter once will be again	Recognizes that customer adoption behavior is fluid
Measurement of Success	Prioritizes adoption rates and market penetration as key success metrics	Evaluates success through short and long-term impact, stakeholder alignment, and ecosystem integration
Strategic Implications	Treats adoption as a one-time milestone. Once a market segment adopts, focus shifts elsewhere	Recognizes adoption as dynamic and cyclical, requiring ongoing alignment, adaptation, and refinement over time

Like other foundational frameworks such as the Business Model Canvas and Blue Ocean Strategy, CFOSS transcends traditional business categorizations. But where those models focus on business strategy and competitive differentiation, CFOSS helps address a different challenge by guiding innovators beyond initial interest toward lasting adoption. Getting customers to say yes is only the beginning; helping them integrate, engage with, and champion an innovation takes ongoing effort. The CFOSS principles apply across business-to-business (B2B) and business-to-consumer (B2C) contexts, focusing on the shared goal of addressing customer demands. This universal applicability enables innovators to unlock new opportunities and accelerate adoption by aligning their offerings with the unique needs of their audiences.

Overview of this Book

This book is for founders, innovators, and anyone striving to bridge the gap between innovation and adoption. It helps you master the complexities of early-stage adoption.

Some readers may expect this book to cover every aspect of launching and running a business, from product development to team building and scaling. Though important, those topics fall outside the scope of this book, which centers on the critical challenge of early-stage customer adoption. Rather than serving as a general guide to entrepreneurship, this book provides a structured framework for overcoming adoption barriers. Here's a glimpse of what lies ahead:

Chapter 2: Rethinking Adoption challenges the assumption that speed equals success. This chapter introduces the IAP, distinguishes problem-market fit from problem-solution fit, and unpacks the five CFOSS pillars.

Chapter 3: Introduction to CFOSS Customer Archetypes dives into the behaviors, mindsets, and decision patterns of CFOSS customer types. Each archetype plays a unique role in the adoption process, and this chapter equips innovators with the insight and tools needed to engage them effectively.

Chapter 4: Unveiling the Layers of CFOSS Value explores how value takes shape across each CFOSS dimension. Readers learn how to construct value propositions that reflect what customers truly care about.

Chapter 5: The Hazards of Mismatching reveals what happens when value propositions miss the mark. Through real-world examples, this chapter surfaces common adoption pitfalls and offers practical strategies to recalibrate and regain traction when progress stalls.

Chapter 6: Mastering Your CFOSS Symphony brings everything together. From enterprise settings to emerging markets, this chapter shows how CFOSS and the IAP can be applied in diverse contexts. Readers walk away with a strategic playbook to turn insight into action and advantage into adoption.

Before we break down CFOSS further, we first need to examine the difference between problem-solution fit and product-market fit. Many promising innovations fail not because they don't work but because they don't align with the market forces that determine adoption.

In chapter 2, we explore why adoption is as much about positioning as it is about performance and how understanding this gap paves the way to real solutions.

What is one key insight from this chapter that changes how you think about customer adoption?

CHAPTER 1 IN REVIEW

- » Startups fail when they don't align with market needs. Nearly half of failures stem from misalignment, not product quality.
- » Transformative ideas struggle without clear communication and alignment with customer priorities.
- » Traditional approaches, like TALC, oversimplify adoption, ignore customer complexity, and miss insights from nonadopters.
- » Common pitfalls in adoption:
  - o Customer hesitation prolongs decisions, stalling revenue and stretching runway.
  - o Delays increase marketing and sales spend, raising burn rate.
  - o Leads show interest but fail to convert, revealing misaligned value propositions.
  - o Early adopters disengage due to unmet expectations or shifting priorities.
  - o Low traction and missed projections make sustaining operations difficult.
  - o Inconsistent metrics and adoption struggles reduce investor confidence.
  - o Workflow, cultural, or regulatory misfits force teams back to the drawing board.
  - o Lack of traction limits access to capital, but funding is needed to gain traction.
- » CFOSS introduces five dimensions for crafting multi-dimensional value propositions:
  - o Core: Solve fundamental problems.
  - o Financial: Highlight ROI and cost savings.
  - o Operational: Ensure seamless integration.
  - o Strategic: Enable differentiation and growth.
  - o Social: Build trust and align with shared values.

Scan to watch the Chapter Overview Video.
Get a quick summary, key insights, and what to look for in the upcoming chapter.

CHAPTER 02

We aimed for the heart and hit the prostate.
–Lonnie Smith, the former president and CEO of Intuitive Surgical

Rethinking Adoption

Many startups and innovators assume that building a superior solution guarantees market success. But in reality, early-stage adoption hurdles are rarely mere execution failures. They stem from a deeper paradox where problem-solution fit and product-market fit are not the same.

When Solutions Don't Sell Themselves

Imagine crafting the perfect key. One that is beautifully designed, expertly engineered, and capable of unlocking even the most complex mechanism. That's problem-solution fit. A well-designed answer to a clearly defined problem. But now, you stand in a vast marketplace, searching for the right door. That's product-market fit. The ability to connect your solution with the right audience in a way that leads to broad adoption.

Conventional wisdom suggests that if you solve a real problem, customers should naturally adopt your innovation. Yet many innovators discover, often painfully, that this isn't the case.

This paradox explains why some of the most technically advanced solutions fail to gain traction, even as less sophisticated products dominate. The following table highlights the critical differences between these two concepts

Aspect	Problem-Solution Fit	Product-Market Fit
Definition	The degree to which an innovation effectively solves a problem	The alignment between the innovation and market demand
Key Focus	Functionality, performance, and technical problem-solving	Adoption, market readiness, and customer behavior
Primary Challenge	Developing a high-quality solution	Gaining market acceptance and demand
Success Indicator	The solution effectively addresses the intended problem	Customers actively adopt and integrate the solution
Common Pitfall	Assuming technical excellence guarantees success	Overlooking whether customers actually need or value it

The da Vinci Surgical System: A Tale of Two Markets

The da Vinci Surgical System offers a striking illustration of this paradox. It was originally developed to transform cardiothoracic surgery by enabling less invasive procedures. Traditional open-heart surgery required cutting through the sternum, leading to longer recovery times, higher infection risks, and increased surgical complexity.[4] In theory, robotic surgery provided a revolutionary alternative, promising smaller incisions, greater precision, and reduced patient trauma.

Robotic-assisted instruments offered delicate movements beyond human capability, paired with 3D magnification that far surpassed traditional surgical loupes. Yet despite these advantages, most cardiothoracic surgeons weren't adopting the technology

The reasons went beyond skepticism. These specialists had spent years mastering traditional techniques, and robotic surgery required a steep learning curve. Some studies suggested it could take one thousand or more cases to achieve proficiency. In an already high-stakes environment, many surgeons saw the risks of transitioning as outweighing the benefits.

Even as some pioneers championed the technology, adoption stalled.

The robotic system solved a critical surgical problem, but it didn't fit within the reality of how cardiothoracic surgeons worked. Hospitals hesitated to invest in a technology that didn't immediately align with surgeon behavior, team logistics, and financial incentives.

The breakthrough for robotic surgery didn't come from where it was expected. Instead, adoption took off in an entirely different market. Robotic prostatectomies and hysterectomies became the key drivers of success.[5] These procedures typically involved smaller teams and already incorporated some minimally invasive techniques, which made the transition to robotics far more natural. The workflows adapted more easily, the learning curve was less severe, and the benefits, such as reduced recovery times and patient preference for less invasive options, were immediately apparent. Hospitals saw competitive advantages and increased demand, and the financial case became clear. What changed? Not the technology, but the alignment between the innovation and the needs of the market.

Aspect	Cardiothoracic Surgery (Initial Market)	Hysterectomies & Prostatectomies (Successful Pivot)
Market Readiness	Resistant. Surgeons were trained in open procedures and hesitant to adopt new workflows.	Receptive. Smaller surgical teams, lower complexity, and some experience with minimally invasive techniques facilitated adoption.
Training & Workflow Impact	Extensive. Required a steep learning curve (hundreds of procedures for mastery), disrupting established workflows.	Moderate. Existing experience with minimally invasive techniques helped streamline the transition to robotics.
Financial Justification	Weak. High costs with uncertain ROI due to slow adoption and low procedure volumes.	Strong. Hospitals saw competitive advantages, increased procedure demand, and improved patient outcomes, justifying investment.
Adoption Rate	Slow. High complexity and workflow disruptions created barriers to widespread uptake.	Faster. Aligned with market needs, patient demand, and existing workflows, leading to rapid adoption.
Alignment	Weaker alignment. High clinical potential but lacked incentives for early adoption.	Stronger alignment. Matched the needs of physicians and hospital decision-makers.

A Modern Cautionary Tale: Microsoft Zune vs. Apple iPod

The paradox of problem-solution fit vs. product-market fit spans industries and applies in both B2B and B2C environments. From enterprise solutions to consumer tech, countless innovations have struggled or thrived based not on technical merit alone but on their alignment with market dynamics. For example, Tesla faced early challenges not because of its cars' capabilities alone, but because consumers also considered factors like charging infrastructure, resale value, and the overall risks associated with being early adopters.

Similarly, in the consumer tech space, Microsoft Zune's failure stemmed not from product quality but from missing the broader ecosystem that made the iPod indispensable. Let's consider how Microsoft Zune and Apple iPod represent two very different outcomes in consumer technology.[6]

Microsoft Zune: Technically Strong, Market Weak

In 2006, Microsoft introduced the Zune, a digital music player designed to compete with Apple's iPod. The Zune featured a larger screen, wireless sharing, and a music subscription service, offering clear technological advantages over the iPod. Yet, despite these strengths, it failed to gain traction.

The problem wasn't the technology. What it lacked was a fit with how consumers actually behaved and what the market demanded. Apple had already cultivated a seamless ecosystem through iTunes, making it effortless for users to manage their music. More than a device, the iPod captured emotion and simplicity in a way that reshaped how we connect with music. Microsoft, by contrast, struggled to create a compelling reason for users to switch.

Much like the da Vinci system's initial focus on cardiothoracic surgery, Zune demonstrated technical superiority but failed to overcome market inertia. These examples drive home an important point. Even with strong problem-solution fit, adoption can stall when the broader context is overlooked.

Apple iPod: Success Through Ecosystem Alignment

The iPod, launched in 2001, wasn't the most advanced MP3 player on the market, but it was the one that nailed product-market fit. Apple's edge came from seamless usability, not technical specs. The iPod's intuitive interface, sleek design, and deep integration with iTunes created an extremely smooth experience for users.[7]

Apple understood that consumers weren't looking for a music player. They wanted a simple way to access and manage their digital music libraries. By aligning technology with actual user behaviors, Apple transformed the iPod from just another device into a cultural icon.

This mirrors the da Vinci system's shift to robotic hysterectomies. Its original cardiothoracic application struggled, but hysterectomies posed fewer operational hurdles and aligned more closely with hospitals' financial and strategic goals. Both cases demonstrate that even disruptive innovations must integrate into the practical realities of their market to succeed.

Microsoft Zune vs. Apple iPod – Competing Strategies

Aspect	Microsoft Zune	Apple iPod
Core Product Offering	High-quality MP3 player with advanced features like wireless sharing	Simplified MP3 player optimized for ease of use
Ecosystem Support	Weak. Lacked a seamless platform for content management.	Strong. Integrated with iTunes for effortless syncing and purchasing.
Market Positioning	Competed on specs but lacked emotional resonance	Created an aspirational brand and lifestyle identity
Adoption Outcome	Failed. Technically strong but lacked market pull.	Thrived. Aligned with user behavior and cultural trends.

Can you recall a product or service that had clear value but still failed to catch on? What non-functional factors might have undermined its success?

The CFOSS® Connection

The contrasting paths of Zune, iPod, and the da Vinci system highlight why successful adoption requires more than technical excellence. Microsoft's Zune and the da Vinci's initial cardiac focus excelled in the core dimension. They were technically superior solutions to real problems. But both struggled because they failed to align with other critical CFOSS dimensions:

» **Strategic Misalignment:** The Zune lacked a compelling brand narrative or integration with existing consumer habits, whereas Apple built an entire ecosystem around iTunes.

» **Social Disconnect:** Microsoft failed to cultivate a community or brand identity around Zune. In contrast, Apple turned the iPod into a cultural symbol of innovation and self-expression.

» **Operational Resistance:** Early robotic cardiac procedures disrupted hospital workflows and required extensive retraining, limiting their appeal to surgeons and administrators.

By contrast, the iPod and da Vinci's hysterectomy success illustrate strong CFOSS alignment:

» **Financial:** The iPod was perceived as a high-value product at a justifiable price, and da Vinci hysterectomies generated strong hospital ROI.

» **Operational:** iTunes made music management effortless, and robotic hysterectomies integrated more smoothly into surgical workflows.

» **Social:** The iPod became a catalyst for the digital music revolution, shifting how communities accessed and shared music. Likewise, robotic hysterectomies allowed women to return to their families and work faster.

True adoption requires a multi-dimensional approach.

A Framework for Innovation Adoption

In 2012, the paradox of robotic gallbladder surgery adoption in hospitals sparked a journey that reshaped my understanding of innovation adoption. Despite limited evidence that robotics improved minimally invasive gallbladder outcomes or justified higher costs, hospitals were still investing heavily in this robotic-assisted procedure.[8] On the surface, this seemed to contradict the healthcare industry's emphasis on evidence-based medicine and value-driven care. So what hidden forces were influencing these decisions?

As I dug deeper, it became clear that this pattern wasn't unique to healthcare. In industries as diverse as renewable energy, transportation, and manufacturing, organizations faced similar struggles when integrating transformative technologies. They weren't simply evaluating whether an innovation worked. They were weighing how it fit into their financial goals, operational realities, strategic positioning, and broader stakeholder relationships. From this insight, CFOSS was born.

CFOSS pillars each contribute uniquely to shaping adoption success.

Like a hand at work, they function in concert. Each finger plays a distinct role, yet together they achieve a firm grip. In the same way, CFOSS gives innovators the dexterity to grasp the complexities of adoption. It safeguards businesses from overreliance on any single factor by aligning multiple dimensions to generate meaningful traction. This integrated approach helps innovators anticipate challenges, seize opportunities, and maintain alignment between their innovation and real-world market dynamics.

The Core Pillar: The Rooted Foundation

Understanding the Core Pillar

The Core Pillar serves as the foundation of every innovation. Like the roots of a tree, it provides stability, nourishment, and direction. It defines your organization's identity, purpose, and fundamental reason for existing. More than a set of attributes, the Core Pillar shapes why you innovate, creating long-term alignment across financial sustainability, operational efficiency, strategic positioning, and stakeholder engagement.

A strong Core Pillar guides not simply what you create but also why it matters. It connects with customers, employees, and partners, fostering trust and longevity. Without a well-defined core, innovations risk being disjointed, short lived, or easily commoditized.

Beyond Features and Benefits

The Core Pillar doesn't focus on product features alone but on the purpose that drives them. A company committed to sustainability, for example, offers more than eco-friendly products. It builds an entire business around environmental responsibility and ethical practices, as seen with Patagonia. A tech company focused on innovation does more than develop software. It fosters a culture of continuous advancement and reinvention, like Apple.

Simon Sinek's *Start with Why* captures the essence of the Core Pillar. It is the deep-rooted purpose that motivates action and creates loyalty.

The Thumb Principle: Why the Core Pillar Is Foundational

Within CFOSS, the Core Pillar functions like the thumb. The only opposable digit. Its unique ability to directly touch every other finger head-on mirrors how the Core Pillar connects with and influences every other dimension of innovation: financial, operational, strategic, and social.

Just as the thumb enables grip, stability, and coordination, the Core Pillar holds the entire framework together. It is the anchor that keeps an organization's innovation efforts from becoming disconnected, temporary, or interchangeable.

Moreover, like a thumbprint distinctive to each individual, the Core Pillar reflects the unique identity of each organization. This foundational element shapes strategy, culture, and decision-making at every level. More than a statement of values, the Core Pillar serves as the organization's pulse.

Principles in Action

Amazon's transformation from an online bookstore to a global tech giant is a prime example of a strong Core Pillar in action. Customer obsession has been its guiding principle, shaping everything from one-click ordering to Prime's convenience-driven ecosystem. This relentless focus on customer-centric innovation has fueled its expansion into retail, cloud computing, and artificial intelligence.

Similarly, the Core Pillar of Starbucks centers not on coffee, but on community and experience. Its cafés serve as "third places" between home and work, turning coffee drinking into a social and cultural ritual that fosters worthwhile customer connections.[9]

The power of a clearly defined Core Pillar extends beyond business. Dr. Martin Luther King Jr.'s leadership, as discussed in Chapter 1, was rooted in a simple but transformative Core Pillar grounded in the moral imperative of justice and equality. His vision focused not only on legal reform but on reshaping society's conscience. Dr. King did more than offer solutions to discrimination. He brought people together around a shared purpose, building trust and inspiring action. His "I Have a Dream" speech offered more than words. The message captured the heart of the movement and made people not only listen but truly feel.

In healthcare, leading institutions define their Core Pillar around patient care, ensuring so that every innovation, investment, and operational decision serves the mission of improving lives. Hospitals that embed this core pillar adopt new treatments as part of broader care models that enhance accessibility, empathy, and patient trust.

Applying Core Principles

The strength of the Core Pillar manifests in several critical ways:
- » Acts as a decision-making compass, keeping long-term alignment with mission and values.
- » Fosters connections with stakeholders who share the same purpose
- » Drives innovation in the right direction, so that new developments reinforce, not distract from, the mission
- » Creates synergy across the framework, grounding financial, operational, strategic, and social decisions in core principles
- » Attracts like-minded collaborators and partners

The Financial Pillar: Guarding Fiscal Strength

Understanding the Financial Pillar

The Core Pillar serves as the foundation that propels the business forward and keeps purpose at the center of every decision, whereas the Financial Pillar underpins its economic sustainability. This pillar extends beyond profitability, encompassing fiscal health, long-term stability, and calculated resource allocation. It answers a fundamental question. What is the economic impact of this innovation, and how does it support long-term viability?

A well-managed Financial Pillar creates a stable foundation for growth, enabling businesses to navigate economic uncertainty, invest in the future, and sustain innovation without compromising financial integrity.

Beyond Short-Term Gains

Long-term sustainability demands intentional financial planning, including budgeting, forecasting, and risk management. Successful organizations balance fiscal discipline with investments in technology, talent, and infrastructure. These investments may not yield immediate returns, but they strengthen financial stability, improve cash flow management, and build the runway needed for sustained growth.

The Index Finger Principle: Pinching Pennies & Pointing the Way Forward

The Financial Pillar aligns with the index finger, which points the way forward and guides precision tasks. The Financial Pillar ensures that economic decisions remain sustainable and aligned with the Core Pillar.

The thumb and index finger don't just point. They pinch, grasp, and refine. Financial decisions require deliberate control, whether it's watching costs to maintain fiscal responsibility or making targeted investments that strengthen long-term sustainability. An organization that fails to balance these elements risks either overextending financially or missing opportunities for growth.

Principles in Action

Amazon's Financial Pillar focuses on balancing profitability with strategic investments. Amazon reinvests in technology, infrastructure, and market expansion to drive long-term growth and maintain financial flexibility. Through disciplined capital allocation, it scales efficiently and sustains its competitive edge.

Starbucks similarly leverages financial discipline to fuel its mission of community and connection. Menu innovation, loyalty programs, and operational efficiency help optimize revenue without compromising premium quality or brand experience.

The Montgomery Bus Boycott exemplifies financial strategy as a tool for systemic change. Civil rights leaders balanced economic pressure with financial sustainability, raising funds, and leveraging community support to sustain the movement. By disrupting the revenue model of Montgomery's transit system, heavily reliant on Black ridership, they forced institutional change, proving that financial leverage can drive social transformation.

In healthcare, the Financial Pillar plays a crucial role in balancing cost management with patient outcomes. Hospitals must navigate reimbursement challenges, technology investments, and budget constraints, to remain financially stable without compromising quality of care.

Applying Financial Principles

The Financial Pillar strengthens organizations by:
- » Providing a clear framework for financial viability and ROI
- » Directing resources to high-potential initiatives and steering clear of unsustainable ventures
- » Driving growth through a balance of immediate profitability and long-term investments
- » Maintaining fiscal discipline by analyzing financial trends and managing risks proactively

Much like the index finger provides precision and control, the Financial Pillar guides resource allocation to balance short-term stability and long-term economic sustainability.

The Operational Pillar: The Engine of Efficiency

Understanding the Operational Pillar

The Operational Pillar focuses on how innovations integrate into an organization's existing workflows and processes. It is the engine of efficiency, turning innovation from a great idea into a practical, scalable solution. By addressing the critical question of how, the Operational Pillar transforms concepts into actionable strategies that fit seamlessly into the user's daily reality.

More than optimizing workflows, the Operational Pillar fosters a culture of continuous improvement. It enhances productivity by refining processes, reducing inefficiencies, and leveraging technology, not only to cut costs but to empower teams to execute with precision. When properly implemented, this pillar creates stability without stagnation, allowing businesses to adapt and grow without disrupting core functions.

Beyond Process Integration

Operational excellence ensures seamless coordination between processes, technology, and people. True efficiency isn't measured solely by speed or cost reduction but by how well an organization integrates improvements into its daily operations without disruption.

The most effective organizations embed operational excellence into their culture, ensuring that efficiency gains are both sustainable and scalable. When operations run smoothly, organizations become more agile, better equipped to adapt to challenges, and capable of delivering consistent value over time.

The Middle Finger Principle

The Operational Pillar is best represented by the middle finger, standing tall, providing steadiness, and maintaining balance across the organization. As the middle finger helps stabilize the hand's grip, the Operational Pillar connects and strengthens all other CFOSS pillars, helping processes, teams, and technologies work in unison.

And yes, when misused, the middle finger can send the wrong message. Operational rigidity can alienate teams, slow down innovation, and create unnecessary friction. A well-run operation keeps workflows smooth, adaptable, and aligned with broader organizational goals rather than becoming a source of frustration.

Principles in Action

Amazon's logistics network is a top example of operational excellence, optimizing order fulfillment, inventory management, and delivery speeds while maintaining alignment with its customer-centric mission.[10] The company's ability to scale operations without compromising service highlights how the Operational Pillar supports long-term value creation.

Starbucks integrates operations into the customer experience through standardized workflows that preserve a personal touch.[11] Its ability to optimize efficiency, without losing sight of hospitality, demonstrates how the Operational Pillar enhances both productivity and engagement.

The Montgomery Bus Boycott showcased operational excellence through a meticulously organized carpool system that allowed thousands to commute despite the absence of public transportation. Leaders coordinated routes, volunteer drivers, and support hubs, sustaining the boycott for more than a year. This logistical precision kept the movement running, proving that efficient operations aren't only a matter of productivity. They're essential for sustaining large-scale change.

In healthcare, hospitals apply operational principles to streamline patient care, reducing wait times, optimizing treatment workflows, and leveraging technology for seamless coordination between departments. These improvements drive both clinical efficiency and patient outcomes, reinforcing how operational strength influences long-term success.

Applying Operational Principles

The Operational Pillar drives execution through several key practices:
- » Facilitating seamless integration of new initiatives into existing workflows
- » Coordinating cross-functional collaboration for streamlined execution
- » Maintaining stability and quality control without sacrificing adaptability
- » Embedding continuous improvement to refine processes over time
- » Designing systems that scale efficiently

The Operational Pillar promotes harmony across organizational processes, allowing for the efficient execution of day-to-day operations and new initiatives.

The Strategic Pillar: Securing Long-Term Advantage

Understanding the Strategic Pillar

The Strategic Pillar helps align innovation with both short-term advantage and long-term market viability. It defines where an organization stands within its industry, how it differentiates itself, and how it builds enduring value. Whether through technological superiority, unique positioning, or addressing an under-served segment, a strong strategic foundation not only fuels present momentum but also shapes future trajectory.

The Strategic Pillar orchestrates long-term positioning, guiding organizations through industry shifts, competitive threats, and emerging opportunities. Companies that master this pillar shape the market landscape and proactively influence how industries evolve.

Beyond Traditional Strategic Thinking

Traditional strategy often prioritizes market share, cost leadership, or differentiation, but the Strategic Pillar challenges these conventional metrics. Short-term wins are important, but sustainable leadership comes from anticipating industry shifts, fostering innovation, and aligning strategically with future opportunities. Organizations that rely solely on incremental improvements often find themselves outpaced by competitors who think past immediate gains.

A well-structured strategy blends near-term execution with long-term positioning, ensuring that companies don't just adapt to change but drive it. The key isn't simply competing today. It's securing your place in the industry's future by investing in durable competitive advantages and cultivating strategic flexibility.

The Ring Finger Principle

The ring finger symbolizes commitment, endurance, and positioning. These attributes are key to crafting a sound strategy. A ring represents enduring commitment. In the same way, strategy defines an organization's industry position and reinforces its long-term resilience and competitiveness. A well-crafted strategy is not static; it requires ongoing refinement, balancing short-term competitive advantages with lasting market differentiation.

Principles in Action

The acquisition of Instagram exemplifies strategic excellence by Meta, as the company leveraged Instagram's growing influence to strengthen its position in social media. Meta's integration of Instagram expanded its audience and strengthened community building, positioning the company for sustained leadership in the mobile-first digital age.[12]

Amazon's pursuit of innovation has helped it become "the everything store," uniting advanced technology, an extensive product range, and a seamless customer experience to sustain its competitive edge.[13] Its strategic emphasis on long-term growth enables it to anticipate market shifts, navigate complexities, and reinforce its leadership across multiple industries.

Netflix's pivot from DVD rentals to streaming redefined the entertainment industry. Recognizing the shift toward digital consumption before competitors, Netflix strategically transitioned its business model, investing heavily in original content and data-driven recommendations. This forward-thinking approach allowed it to outmaneuver traditional media companies and establish itself as the dominant force in on-demand entertainment.

Dr. King's leadership in the Montgomery Bus Boycott exemplifies strategic excellence in social change. He positioned the boycott not as a protest but as a catalyst for long-term civil rights reform. Dr. King's alignment of the local movement with national legal efforts, economic pressure, and media strategy made the boycott a catalyst for both immediate impact and lasting change. His ability to differentiate the movement as a moral, economic, and legal imperative helped shift public perception and policy, sustaining the civil rights movement's relevance.

Applying Strategic Principles

A strong Strategic Pillar ensures that organizations:
- » Position themselves for sustained growth through differentiation and competitive foresight
- » Build long-term partnerships that expand market presence and create ecosystem advantages
- » Align innovations with future industry trends, ensuring adaptability in an evolving landscape
- » Invest in strategic initiatives that endure beyond short-term market shifts

When integrated with the Core and Operational Pillars, strategy ensures that innovation is not only launched but also sustained and scaled.

The Social Pillar: Weaving a Tapestry of Impact

Understanding the Social Pillar

The Social Pillar focuses on how innovation affects entire ecosystems, including users, communities, industries, and advocacy groups. The Core Pillar focuses on why an innovation exists for a specific individual or customer. While, the Social Pillar considers how it resonates across entire stakeholder groups and social systems.

Unlike models that prioritize financial outcomes alone, the Social Pillar recognizes that long-term business success is strengthened by its relationships with communities. Businesses that integrate this pillar don't serve individual customers. They influence the collective well-being of organizations, networks, and social movements. Whether through sustainability, ethical supply chains, or public health initiatives, companies that prioritize social outcomes create stakeholder trust, expand their influence, and align with the needs of customer communities, not individual consumers.

Beyond Individual Gain

The Social Pillar highlights the broader role of organizations as societal stakeholders. Companies like Warby Parker and Patagonia have demonstrated that embedding social responsibility into their business model strengthens customer devotion. Warby Parker's Buy a Pair, Give a Pair program ties its success to providing eyewear for those in need, reinforcing the brand's mission and expanding its customer base in the process.[14] Similarly, Patagonia's commitment to sustainability, from fair-trade supply chains to its Don't Buy This Jacket campaign, has cultivated a fiercely loyal customer base that values environmental ethics as much as product quality.

These companies exemplify how businesses that genuinely align with societal needs are not only respected but embraced by consumers, creating brand equity and long-term sustainability.

The Pinky Finger Principle

The Social Pillar is represented by the pinky finger is the smallest yet surprisingly powerful digit. Though often overlooked, the pinky contributes up to 50 percent of the hand's grip strength proving that even the smallest components can play a critical role in overall success.[15]

This mirrors the often-underestimated impact of social responsibility in business. When embedded properly, the Social Pillar strengthens an organization's foundation. As the pinky enhances both strength and balance in the hand, the Social Pillar makes a company's success socially meaningful.

Principles in Action

Muhammad Yunus exemplifies social entrepreneurship through Grameen Bank, showing how business methods can tackle social challenges and improve lives at scale. Through microfinance initiatives, Grameen Bank has transformed millions of lives, particularly those of women in rural communities, showing how social innovation can drive systemic change.

Organizations like the American Heart Association (AHA) demonstrate how focused social initiatives can create meaningful change in specific communities. Through targeted programs, major research investments, and public education efforts, they advance cardiovascular health while building strong partnerships across the healthcare ecosystem. A notable example is the AHA's $20 million Health Equity Research Network initiative, which engages communities most impacted by health disparities in developing solutions that enhance overall well-being.[16]

Amazon integrates social value into its business model through initiatives like Amazon Smile and environmental sustainability efforts. These programs may appear small compared to broader operations, yet they deliver vital support to thousands of charitable organizations and environmental initiatives. Similarly, Starbucks reinforces its commitment to ethical sourcing and community development through fair-trade practices and investments in coffee-growing regions, demonstrating how companies can embed social outcomes into their supply chains.

Hospitals fulfill their social mission through community outreach programs and public health initiatives, extending their role beyond patient care to address broader social determinants of health. Meaningful social impact isn't about isolated initiatives or compliance-driven programs. Instead, successful organizations integrate social responsibility into their strategic decisions, aligning outcomes with their long-term vision and business fundamentals.

Applying Social Principles

The Social Pillar demonstrates its impact through:

- » Aligning success with societal progress to support ethical and sustainable business growth
- » Building authentic relationships with communities to foster goodwill and trust
- » Innovating to address social challenges, embedding purpose into business strategy
- » Creating lasting impact beyond financial returns, reinforcing brand reputation and longevity
- » Strengthening organizational purpose so that profit and purpose grow together

The Impact of a Strong Social Pillar

Like the pinky finger's unexpected contribution to grip strength, the Social Pillar plays a vital but often underestimated role in business success. Integrating the Social Pillar into the broader CFOSS framework helps organizations shape innovations that serve both customer needs and community well-being. The most successful businesses recognize that profit and purpose are not opposing forces. They reinforce each other as essential drivers of transformation.

Now, we can see how each pillar offers a critical lens for evaluating how an innovation reflects internal priorities and responds to external market realities. Figure 2.1: The CFOSS Five-Finger Model illustrates how the five pillars of innovation adoption function like the fingers of a hand, each playing a vital role in achieving successful alignment

Figure 2.1: The CFOSS Five-Finger Model illustrates how the five pillars of innovation adoption function like the fingers of a hand, each playing a vital role in achieving successful alignment.

Thumb (Core)
• Coordinates with all other fingers
• Essential for alignment and purpose

Index Finger (Financial)
• Points the way
• Financial considerations often drive direction

Middle Finger (Operational)
• Key to sustainable implementation
• Efficiency driven

Ring Finger (Strategic)
• Represents commitment
• Ideal for aligning with early adopters

Pinky Finger (Social)
• Adds essential strength
• Social impact is crucial for momentum

To summarize, the CFOSS pillars table below captures the essential purpose of each pillar, the key adoption question it addresses, and examples of how industry leaders have applied these principles successfully.

CFOSS Pillars

CFOSS Pillar	Definition	Key Question It Answers	Example in Action
Core (Thumb)	The fundamental reason an innovation exists. Its essential purpose and problem-solving capability	Why does this innovation matter?	Amazon: Customer obsession drives everything from marketplace strategy to the Alexa ecosystem.
Financial (Index Finger)	The economic impact, including return on investment, cost considerations, and long-term viability	How much financial value does this innovation create?	Netflix: The subscription model generates recurring revenue and maintains attractive pricing to retain customers.
Operational (Middle Finger)	The efficiency, scalability, and process integration of an innovation within existing workflows	How does this innovation fit into current systems and processes?	Tesla: Streamlined supply chains and direct-to-consumer sales revolutionized auto industry operations.
Strategic (Ring Finger)	The long-term positioning, competitive differentiation, and market sustainability of an innovation	Where does this innovation position the organization within its industry?	Apple: Ecosystem approach (iPhone + App Store) locks in customer loyalty.
Social (Pinky Finger)	The broader impact on communities, societal well-being, and stakeholder engagement	Who benefits from this innovation on a collective level?	Patagonia: Pioneers environmental sustainability in fashion through fair trade and recycled materials.

CFOSS Industry Application Table

The principles of CFOSS apply across products, industries, and eras. Whether leading a global tech firm, building a consumer brand, driving a social movement, or transforming healthcare, the challenge remains the same. Innovators must ensure their solutions reflect what customers genuinely need and value. To illustrate this versatility, the table below explores how CFOSS shows up in diverse contexts. From Amazon's logistical precision to Starbucks' cultural influence, from healthcare reform to the strategic brilliance of the Montgomery Bus Boycott.

Organization/ Example	Core (Why?)	Financial (How much?)	Operational (How?)	Strategic (Where?)	Social (Who?)
Amazon	Customer obsession as the foundation for innovation	Company invests heavily in long-term growth, sacrificing short-term profits for market dominance.	Optimized logistics, fulfillment centers, and cloud infrastructure streamline global operations.	Expands across multiple sectors (e-commerce, cloud computing, AI) to reinforce dominance and adaptability	Influences global commerce, impacting suppliers, workers, and entire market ecosystems
Starbucks	Creating a "third place" between home and work, emphasizing community	Premium pricing and loyalty programs drive revenue and uphold high quality standards.	Standardized workflows improve efficiency and still allow for personalized service.	Positions itself as a lifestyle brand, shaping global coffee culture	Supports coffee farmers through ethical sourcing and fair-trade initiatives
Martin Luther King Jr. (Montgomery Bus Boycott)[17]	Challenged systemic injustice by emphasizing dignity and equal rights	Financial pressure on the transit system forced policy change and helped sustain the movement's operations.	Organized carpools and community-driven alternatives maintained participation.	Strategically framed the boycott as a national civil rights battle, leveraging legal challenges and media to drive systemic change	Unified communities, creating long-term shifts in societal attitudes and legal frameworks
Healthcare Industry	Patient-centered care as the foundation for medical advancements	Balances cost efficiency with access, reimbursement models, and innovation investments.	Streamlined workflows improve patient outcomes and hospital efficiency.	Balances innovation with policy, regulation, and industry forces to drive long-term healthcare transformation	Addresses public health challenges, improving community wellness and access to care

Innovation Fit to Customer Adoption

At this point you have the tools to assess the CFOSS implications of any innovation, whether you are evaluating an existing product, considering a new venture, or refining an offering to enhance adoption. However, understanding CFOSS at an innovation level is only part of the equation.

In chapter 3, we shift focus from evaluating innovation to understanding CFOSS-driven customer characteristics. A core-driven customer prioritizes different factors than a social-driven customer. A financial-oriented buyer won't weigh adoption decisions the same way as an operationally motivated one. In breaking down CFOSS customer archetypes, we'll explore how different customers approach innovation, what drives their decisions, and how recognizing these patterns helps businesses anticipate and overcome adoption barriers.

CHAPTER 2 IN REVIEW

» The Innovation Adoption Pathway demonstrates that even a superior problem-solution fit doesn't guarantee market success.

» The CFOSS framework provides a structured approach to bridging the gap between problem-solution fit and market success, encompassing five essential pillars:
  o Core: Defines fundamental purpose and problem-solving capability (why)
  o Financial: Assesses economic impact and long-term viability (how much)
  o Operational: Ensures process integration and efficiency (how)
  o Strategic: Establishes long-term market positioning and differentiation (where)
  o Social: Evaluates broader community impact and societal alignment (who)

» Each CFOSS pillar corresponds to a finger on the hand, symbolizing its distinct role in securing adoption success in the Five-Finger Model:
  o Thumb (Core): Provides foundational grip, enabling all other functions
  o Index Finger (Financial): Points to opportunities and signals economic viability
  o Middle Finger (Operational): Balances and stabilizes execution
  o Ring Finger (Strategic): Represents long-term commitment and market positioning
  o Pinky Finger (Social): Enhances overall balance and support, despite being often overlooked

Scan to watch the Chapter Overview Video.
Get a quick summary, key insights, and what to look for in the upcoming chapter.

CHAPTER 03

The greatest compliment that was ever paid me was when someone asked me what I thought, and attended to my answer.
—Henry David Thoreau

Introduction to CFOSS® Customer Archetypes

In this chapter, we will dive into the distinct customer types whose behaviors, values, and needs align with each CFOSS pillar. Recognizing these archetypes empowers innovators to design offerings that feel relevant and meaningful to their intended audiences.

Later, we'll discuss how to craft clear promises of value that speak directly to the needs of these archetypes. But in order to design effective value propositions, we need to first understand who our customers are and what matters most to them.

Each pillar corresponds to a customer archetype, remember the hand analogy we discussed in the previous chapter. The thumb (core) represents Problem Pioneers, who push innovation with their insights into the primary challenges. The index finger (financial) directs attention to

Fiscal Architects, who validate the financial viability of innovations. The middle finger (operational) refers to Productivity Gurus, who focus on seamless integration into existing systems. The ring finger (strategic) symbolizes Visionary Trailblazers, who look ahead, prioritizing competitive advantage. Finally, the pinky finger (social) signifies Network Ambassadors, who elevate community well-being and collective progress.

Understanding these archetypes is crucial because, like a hand drawing strength and control from all five fingers, successful market adoption depends on engaging and aligning with each distinct customer type. Exploring each archetype in depth reveals how to meet customer needs and design offerings that truly resonate.

Why Understanding CFOSS Customers Matters

Without an understanding of CFOSS customer archetypes, value propositions risk missing the mark. They may fail to connect with the priorities of those they aim to serve.

Here's a simple analogy. Imagine a startup founder who is passionate about creating a product that solves a specific problem for a niche market. She finds purpose and fulfillment in the challenge of developing a solution and getting it to customers. Meanwhile, a potential investor sees the same product as a risky venture, finding it too unproven or too focused on a small audience. This contrast illustrates a crucial truth. Value is subjective. What excites one individual may seem like an impractical or unnecessary risk to another. Similarly, businesses must recognize that customers perceive and prioritize value in unique ways.

Using these archetypes, innovators can align their strategies with customer needs and avoid the pitfalls discussed earlier in the book. We begin with core customers. The Problem Pioneers whose immersion in the challenge space propels innovation forward. These are the customers who not only identify issues but also seek to actively shape solutions.

Core Customer: Problem Pioneers

As the thumb enables the hand to function through its grip, core customers drive innovation by fully engaging with the problem and actively pursuing solutions. These Problem Pioneers are not mere users of products. They actively contribute to refining and shaping solutions, offering critical insights that propel innovation forward.

Understanding the Core Customer

Core customers form the foundation of successful early adoption. They aren't casual enthusiasts. They're Problem Pioneers with a personal connection to the challenges your solution addresses. Their expertise comes from firsthand experience.

As illustrated by the evolution of robotic surgery adoption, Dr. Randy Chitwood, Dr. Douglas Murphy, Dr. Vip Patel, and Dr. Gerald Feuer played key roles in shaping the technology's applications. These core customers were not passive adopters of new technology but active participants in its development. Their involvement extended beyond using the robotic system. They carefully tracked procedural challenges and provided essential feedback that helped improve the technology. For example, Dr. Chitwood was known for his detailed notes on how the robotic arms could improve precision in cardiac surgeries. Dr. Patel led efforts to adjust the system to improve patient positioning in prostate surgeries. Dr. Feuer helped design specialized tools for gynecologic oncology procedures, offering sketches and detailed input on the movements needed. This level of engagement from hands-on experience to thoughtful refinement was what made them Problem Pioneers. They adopted the technology and worked relentlessly to shape it around real-world clinical needs, ultimately guiding its trajectory and transforming it into an essential tool for modern surgery.

Core customers occupy a critical space in market entry by not only validating innovations but through valuable feedback and early use. These customers are unique in their combination of expertise and emotional investment. Unlike occasional users or casual observers, they immerse themselves in the problem and proposed solutions, driven by a profound desire to create meaningful change. Their relationship with the challenge goes beyond professional curiosity. They view it as a mission aligned with their core values and purpose.

Core customers meticulously track their experiences, whether through detailed documentation or mental notes. They focus on both successes and failures, using these observations to refine their approach to solving the problem. Many participate in networks or communities dedicated to addressing challenges, sharing insights and learning from others. This thoughtful engagement makes them invaluable partners in bridging the gap between theoretical solutions and practical applications.

However, this expertise can also make core customers particularly demanding. Their high standards stem from having seen multiple solutions fail. They remain open to innovation, but their healthy skepticism allows only the most thoughtful and impactful solutions to earn their trust.

Core customers are not merely early adopters but critical enablers of success. According to Everett Rogers's Diffusion of Innovation theory, early adopters embrace new ideas early, motivated by curiosity, personal benefits, and social influence.[18] These individuals often act as opinion leaders, helping to legitimize innovations for a broader audience.

Though core customers share certain traits with early adopters, their underlying motivations are distinct. Early adopters are typically driven by a general interest in exploring new technologies. In contrast, core customers are entrenched in the problem itself. Their engagement stems from a personal or professional stake in overcoming specific challenges, making them naturally inclined to participate in developing and refining solutions.

This level of involvement makes core customers key players in helping innovations move from early adoption to the mainstream. A central idea in Geoffrey Moore's *Crossing the Chasm*.[19] By validating solutions through their expertise and credibility, core customers provide the critical momentum needed to transition innovations from problem-solution fit to product-market fit. Their contributions not only enhance the practical relevance of solutions but also foster confidence among broader audiences. When organizations recognize and build on the distinct strengths of core customers, they lay the groundwork for strategies that drive lasting growth.

Case Study: Tackling Hospital-Acquired Infections

The essence of a core customer came to life in the story of an infection preventionist I met while helping hospitals reduce hospital-acquired infection (HAI) rates. Before the COVID-19 pandemic, I met a nurse who had spent years relentlessly addressing hospital-acquired infections. Her deep commitment and firsthand understanding exemplified the essence of a core customer.

HAIs pose a significant challenge, affecting one in thirty-one hospital patients and costing US hospitals at least $28 billion annually.[20] For this nurse, however, these weren't abstract statistics. They represented real people facing prolonged hospital stays, poorer outcomes, and preventable deaths. She wasn't just doing her job. This was a mission shaped by personal conviction.

When we first met, she presented a well-worn notebook filled with meticulous records of interventions she had tried over the years. More than a list of failed attempts, it stood as a testament to her relentless commitment to solving a critical healthcare problem. Despite years of frustration, her passion and resolve remained undiminished. Her frequent "Have you thought about this?" interjections demonstrated both her expertise and her eagerness to contribute to the development of effective solutions.

Her defining quality as a quintessential core customer wasn't merely her understanding of the problem. It was her ability to envision comprehensive solutions that addressed challenges holistically. Once she saw potential in our proposed approach, she became an advocate. She facilitated crucial conversations with hospital leadership, championed the implementation process, and helped align stakeholders behind the solution.

This story encapsulates the three defining characteristics of core customers:

1. Deep Problem Connection: Core customers have a profound understanding of the problem, often gained through direct and prolonged experience.
2. Active Engagement: They are proactive participants in developing and refining solutions rather than passive observers.
3. Solution Partnership: When they identify promising innovations, they actively work to implement and advocate for them, becoming partners in their adoption.

Core customers provide the essential foundation for successful innovation adoption. Their in-depth understanding of the problem and their willingness to engage in solution development make them invaluable allies in bridging the gap between innovation and successful market adoption.

Core Customer Behaviors and Expressions

Core customers differentiate themselves not only through their connection to problems but also through their diverse behaviors and characteristic expressions. These behaviors are consistent patterns that reflect their expertise, persistence, and commitment to finding effective solutions.

The most revealing behaviors of core customers often emerge during early discussions about potential solutions. When a core customer says, "Let me try it," they're not merely expressing curiosity; they are signaling their belief that direct experimentation is crucial for evaluating the feasibility of an innovation. Having experienced numerous solutions that looked promising on paper but failed in practice, core customers prioritize firsthand engagement as an indispensable step in assessing a solution's potential.

Their expertise becomes most evident during moments of collaboration. When they interject with, "Here's something you haven't considered," it usually introduces a thoughtful observation rooted in years of personal experience. These contributions often highlight subtle complexities of implementation or unexpected interdependencies that others may overlook. Such insights are invaluable, as they help identify and address potential obstacles early in the development process.

Core customers often exhibit a unique persistence in seeking solutions. They ask challenging, forward-thinking questions like, "What happens when we scale this?" or "How will this address exceptional scenarios?" These questions demonstrate their focus not only on immediate problem-solving but also on long-term sustainability and adaptability. Their persistence can sometimes come across as demanding, but it stems from a desire for solutions that are robust and well-integrated.

Another hallmark of core customers is their tendency to share knowledge generously. Their statements often start with, "Did you know you could . . ." followed by practical tips that bridge the gap between theory and application. These insights aren't casual advice. They represent hard-earned lessons from both successes and failures. When core customers share this knowledge, they provide actionable guidance that can prevent costly missteps and accelerate the path to adoption.

As the thumb connects with every finger, core customers bridge across all other types linking financial, operational, strategic, and social perspectives around a shared problem. Their understanding of the problem allows them to bridge gaps and facilitate collaboration across these diverse archetypes. For example, a core customer might highlight a solution's cost-effectiveness to financial stakeholders and offer guidance to operational teams on integrating it effectively into existing workflows. They collaborate with strategic customers to align innovations with long-term market objectives and with social customers to maximize community impact.

Core customers also display a willingness to challenge assumptions, often saying, "Why do we have to do it this way?" or "What if we approached it differently?" These expressions reflect an ability to think critically about entrenched practices and explore new possibilities. Far from obstructive, their skepticism serves to refine solutions, directing attention to root causes over surface-level symptoms.

These behavioral patterns characterize core customers in ways that contrast with other customer types. Other customers might express vague interest with remarks like "That sounds interesting" or "Let me know when it's ready." In contrast, core customers demonstrate immediate, specific engagement. Their responses consistently reflect close familiarity with the problem, not just excitement about new technology.

Unlike early adopters who may focus on the novelty of a solution, core customers ground their interest in practical problem-solving and real-world application.

Tools and Methods for Engagement

Core customers evaluation combines informal ideation with structured evaluation, creating a dynamic environment for refining and advancing potential innovations.

One trait of core customer engagement is their comfort with informal ideation tools. The proverbial "napkin sketch" isn't merely a cliché. It's a practical and often transformative tool for concept exploration.[21] During problem-solving discussions, core customers frequently use quick, informal sketches to illustrate complex ideas or relationships within the problem space. These visual thinking exercises often yield breakthrough insights that might be overlooked in more formalized settings.

Core customers also embrace paper prototypes and rough mockups as critical tools for engagement. They recognize that early-stage concepts don't need to be polished to be meaningful. Instead, they engage with these basic representations, drawing on their direct experience with the problem to envision how rough ideas might evolve into viable solutions. This iterative mindset accelerates development by fostering early feedback and refinement, reducing the risk of committing resources to ideas that lack potential.

When evaluating solutions more formally, core customers employ tools that reflect their systemic understanding of the problem and their commitment to real-life applicability. These tools often include:

» Pilot testing and experimentation, where core customers engage with early versions of the solution to assess its performance in practical, everyday conditions
» Collecting user feedback helps uncover functionality gaps and validate alignment with end-user needs
» Scenario-based assessments, where core customers simulate different situations to test the solution's robustness and adaptability under varying conditions
» Iterative prototyping, using rapid feedback loops to refine and improve the solution based on hands-on testing and continuous evaluation

These methods connect directly to the problem-solution fit. Core customers understand that successful innovations must bridge the gap between theoretical potential and practical application. Their tools and frameworks support this iterative refinement process, helping to uncover and address potential obstacles before they hinder adoption. Through a mix of informal exploration and rigorous analysis, core customers make it possible for innovations to move from concept to practical viability, forming the basis for successful market adoption.

Impact and Value Creation

Core customers play a pivotal role in influencing the sales cycle and reducing customer acquisition costs. Their understanding of the problem makes them credible advocates within their professional networks. When core customers share implementation insights and success stories, their endorsements carry significant weight because they speak from authentic experience, not promotional intent. This peer-to-peer advocacy often resonates more strongly with potential adopters than traditional marketing efforts.

Perhaps most importantly, early engagement with core customers helps organizations avoid the common pitfall of scaling too soon, before achieving true problem-solution fit. Working closely with these customers allows entrepreneurs to build a strong foundation for growth and develop solutions that are both technically advanced and practically useful in real-world contexts. This deliberate, customer-driven approach creates sustainable momentum, laying the groundwork for broader market adoption and long-term success.

Lastly, core customers are instrumental in socializing the solution across the broader customer ecosystem. Their ability to engage and share insights with financial, operational, strategic, and social customers helps prepare the solution for product-market fit. Collaboration with other archetypes enables core customers to support solutions that address a wider range of needs, encouraging broader adoption and commitment.

Core Customer Archetype Profile: The Problem Pioneers

Below is an overview of the core customer archetype and their role in driving innovation.

CATEGORY	DESCRIPTION	EXAMPLE
Key Characteristics	Expertise in problem space. Persistent commitment to finding solutions. Skeptical of unproven claims, yet open to innovation. Personally invested in outcomes.	A seasoned software developer who maintains detailed documentation of software issues and actively experiments with innovative coding solutions
Problem Connection	Combines expertise with emotional investment in the problem space. Views challenges as personal missions rather than just professional obligations.	Surgeons who pioneered minimally invasive techniques, driven by patient outcomes
Typical Behaviors	Proactive statements like "Let me try it," "Here's something you haven't considered," and "Did you know you could . . ." Active engagement in solution development.	A manufacturing engineer sketching process improvements during initial product demonstrations
Preferred Tools	Napkin sketches, paper prototypes, impact analysis frameworks, workflow assessments	A mechanical engineer creating quick 3D-printed models to test ideas for a new assembly line mechanism
Value Creation	Contributes beyond purchasing by providing crucial insights, testing environments, and natural advocacy within professional networks	A logistics manager offering feedback on a prototype delivery tracking system, then championing it within their company
Foundation Role	Like the thumb's grip, provides essential foundation for innovation adoption. Motivated to find practical solutions to a pressing problem.	An automotive mechanic advocating for a better diagnostic tool after years of encountering recurring technical issues

Core customers leave an indelible mark on the innovation process, much like a unique thumbprint that shapes the development of solutions. With both experience and expertise, they offer unmatched value as early-stage collaborators.

However, successful market adoption does not rely solely on core customers. Problem Pioneers help root solutions in meaningful problem-solving, but broader engagement with other customer archetypes is key to achieving wide-scale adoption. Financial customers, whom we'll examine next, bring a different but equally crucial perspective.

> Can you think of a time when customer involvement in testing and feedback helped refine a solution? What did you learn from that process?

Financial Customer: Fiscal Architects

Financial customers focus on the numbers. They assess whether an innovation makes economic sense, asking tough questions about cost, and returns. Their input often determines whether a promising idea gains the traction needed for prolonged success.

Understanding these economic decision-makers enables organizations to craft compelling business cases and avoid the common pitfall of developing technically impressive solutions that lack financial sustainability. They shape not just cost decisions, but also value creation, resource use, and long-term viability.

Understanding the Financial Customer

Financial customers bring precision and clarity to the evaluation of innovations, much like the index finger provides critical direction and focus. These individuals aren't merely budget-conscious gatekeepers—they are analysts who understand that sustainable innovation hinges on sound economic foundations. Their expertise is rooted in balancing the potential of groundbreaking ideas with fiscal responsibility and constraints.

As demonstrated in the adoption of robotic surgery, financial customers, such as hospital CFOs tasked with justifying multi-million-dollar investments, are critical in determining whether innovations can transition from promising concepts to viable market solutions. Their evaluation hinges on their awareness of economic realities and their ability to assess both the short-term and long-term financial implications. For financial customers, the primary concern is whether the innovation can deliver measurable economic value, sustain profitability, and integrate effectively within the organization's budget.

Whereas some customers prioritize features or market trends, financial customers rigorously assess the full spectrum of implementation costs, both visible and hidden. Financial customers help allocate resources, mitigate monetary risks, and position innovations for sustainable growth.

Case Study: The Hidden Costs of Missed Appointments

"Let me tell you about the day that sparked MedTrans Go," Dr. Obi Ugwonali begins, addressing a classroom of eager entrepreneurs in 2024. "I had two surgeries cancelled back-to-back. Not because the patients weren't ready for surgery, but because one couldn't find a ride and the other needed an interpreter." He pauses, letting the gravity of the situation sink in. "Now, think like a hospital CFO. What do you think a cancelled surgery costs?"[22]

Dana Weeks, MedTrans Go's CEO, steps forward, armed with the data that financial customers prioritize. "Each missed appointment costs providers. For specialty care and surgeries, the costs escalate significantly. Nationally, these missed appointments add up to over $150 billion annually. When you're pitching to financial customers, these are the numbers that grab their attention."[23]

"Here's what I learned about financial customers," Dr. Ugwonali continues. "They saw something I initially missed. While I focused on the immediate problem, patients missing appointments, they recognized a complex web of financial implications." Weeks nods, advancing to a slide that consistently captivates hospital CFOs:

» Revenue loss from cancelled procedures
» Wasted operational resources, including preoperative preparation and unused operating room (OR) time
» Idle staff and administrative overhead
» Decline in downstream revenue due to care delays

"When pitching to financial customers," Weeks advises, "you need to speak their language. We're not presenting another scheduling tool. We're offering revenue protection. We're addressing a $150 billion problem that healthcare systems have been treating with Band-Aids."

Dr. Ugwonali elaborates, "Consider the ripple effect. That day, my practice lost significant revenue. The hospital wasted OR time and staff costs. Two patients continued suffering because they couldn't access the care they needed. And all of this happened because of basic logistical issues that could have been resolved for a fraction of the cost."

Weeks emphasizes, "The key lesson about financial customers is that they don't just evaluate your solution. They examine the entire financial ecosystem it impacts. When we show them how solving a $50 transportation issue can protect thousands of dollars in revenue, that's when they truly grasp the value proposition."

She concludes by highlighting the key metrics that matter most to financial customers:

» Reduced cancellations
» Improved resource utilization and staffing
» Better patient satisfaction, leading to improved reimbursement rates

"Remember," Dr. Ugwonali concludes, "financial customers aren't simply looking for solutions. They seek financial validation. They need to see how your innovation translates into tangible economic benefits. That's what transforms an interesting idea into a must-have solution."

As the session ends, Weeks leaves the entrepreneurs with a final thought: "Understanding your financial customer goes beyond knowing their budget constraints. It's about demonstrating how your solution protects and enhances their bottom line." That's what turned MedTrans Go from a good idea into a vital healthcare solution.

Financial Customer Behaviors and Expressions

Financial customers behaviors and inquiries often set them apart from other customer archetypes. During initial solution discussions, financial customers lead with value-driven questions like, "What's the total impact on our bottom line?" Beyond cost alone, they prioritize the broader financial landscape, including ROI, indirect expenses, and sustainability over time. Having encountered many promising solutions that failed to meet financial expectations, they are adept at uncovering hidden costs and risks.

Statements like "Let's break down the total cost of ownership" signal their intent to delve into the financial implications of a solution. This approach uncovers essential factors, such as revenue protection, resource allocation, and scalability, which might be overlooked by other decision-makers.

Fiscal Architects prioritize outcome-driven inquiries, frequently asking, "What's the impact on . . ." followed by areas like cash flow, profitability, or operational costs. These questions reveal their strategic understanding of how innovations influence the broader business economics. Their experience with both successful and failed investments provides invaluable insights that shape the organization's approach to demonstrating financial viability.

What distinguishes financial customers from other archetypes is their unwavering focus on economic impact. Operational customers prioritize implementation. Fiscal Architects anchor their assessments in ROI and measurable outcomes.

Organizations that work closely with financial customers tap into their ability to assess value through data and analysis. Tailoring communication to highlight metrics, ROI, and cost-benefit logic strengthens the case for adoption and surfaces potential concerns early.

Clarifying the Differences Between Financial and Operational Customers

Both financial and operational customers are concerned with resource utilization, but they approach waste from different perspectives. Financial customers focus on how wasted resources, like time, directly affect the economic bottom line. For them, idle time, unused capacity, and delays translate into lost revenue and missed financial opportunities. Their focus is on making sure every dollar spent generates value and strengthens the organization's financial health.

In contrast, operational customers are primarily concerned with how wasted resources influence overall operations. A wasted hour in the OR or an idle staff member doesn't only mean lost revenue. It can disrupt workflow, slow throughput, and create inefficiencies across the system. For operational customers, the goal is to keep operations running smoothly and optimize workflow to meet demand and maintain high levels of service.

In short, financial customers are focused on economic returns, operational customers are focused on operational efficiency. Both perspectives are vital and understanding how to meet the needs of each is key to successful adoption.

Tools and Methods for Engagement

Financial decision-makers rely on a range of analytical tools when evaluating potential investments. Their approach combines quantitative rigor with strategic assessment.

ROI analysis tools form the cornerstone of their evaluation process. These tools help quantify direct costs, indirect financial impacts, and long-term benefits, enabling financial customers to assess resource requirements, revenue projections, and risk-adjusted returns.

Value assessment frameworks consider total cost of ownership, resource optimization potential, and competitive cost structures. These frameworks help provide a clear picture of the innovation's true economic impact.

When performing detailed evaluations, financial customers prioritize methods that assess both short-term viability and long-term sustainability. These include:

» Evaluating cost structure to determine economic viability and scalability of the solution
» Discounted cash flow (DCF) analysis to assess the time value of money and plan future cash flows, factoring in the present value of long-term returns
» Sensitivity analysis to test how changes in key assumptions, such as market conditions or operational costs, affect financial viability
» Net present value (NPV) to calculate the overall value of future returns, helping determine the profitability of investments over time
» Break-even analysis to identify the point at which revenues will cover initial costs, ensuring that investments remain financially feasible
» Customer lifetime value (CLV) vs. customer acquisition cost (CAC) to evaluate the long-term profitability of customer relationships and align acquisition efforts with sustainable revenue generation

These tools and methods allow financial customers to gain a holistic view of the innovation's economic potential.

Impact and Value Creation

Financial customers challenge assumptions around revenue models, cost structures, and market dynamics. When they question pricing strategies or scalability projections, it isn't criticism. It's constructive input. Their perspective helps organizations avoid pursuing business models that may be technically sound but lack long-term financial viability.

This engagement fosters the creation of business-model fit, which differs from problem-solution fit. Core customers validate whether a solution addresses a critical problem. Fiscal Architects assess whether it can be delivered profitably at scale. Business-model fit reflects the ability to deliver customer value alongside sustainable financial returns. This validation encompasses:

- » Revenue models that align with customer willingness to pay
- » Cost structures that enable competitive pricing
- » Resource requirements that scale efficiently
- » Market dynamics that sustain long-term growth

Financial customers play a key role in helping organizations transition from early adoption to broader market acceptance. They shape go-to-market strategies that balance growth ambitions with sustainability imperatives.

Financial Customer Archetype Profile: Fiscal Architects

Financial customers do more than crunch numbers. They shape adoption by validating what's economically viable and sustainable. The table below breaks down their role, mindset, and methods in detail.

CATEGORY	DESCRIPTION	EXAMPLE
Key Characteristics	Expertise in financial analysis Deep expertise in financial analysis and value assessment. Rigorous approach to economic validation. Data-driven decision-making	A CFO in a tech company using financial modeling to analyze capital expenditures, operational costs, and ROI on new software investments
Problem Connection	Combines financial expertise with organizational sustainability goals. Views challenges through the lens of economic viability and long-term profitability	Hospital financial teams analyzing robotic surgery's impact on operating costs and revenue streams
Typical Behaviors	Proactive statements like "Let's look at the numbers," "What's the ROI model?" and "How does this affect our cost structure?" Active engagement in financial validation	A value analysis committee reviewing the financial feasibility of a proposed supply chain optimization tool
Preferred Tools	Financial models, ROI calculators, cost-benefit analyses, resource utilization assessments, comparative financial benchmarks	CFOs using detailed spreadsheets to analyze capital costs, service contracts, and per-case expenses
Value Creation	Plays a pivotal role in shaping adoption by validating economic feasibility, strengthening business models, and grounding value propositions in data	Financial leaders who assess the long-term viability of a proposed IT infrastructure investment and its potential returns
Foundation Role	Like a balance sheet's bottom line, provides essential validation of business viability. Committed to ensuring sustainable economic returns and market success	The materials manager who meticulously analyzes costs and benefits to build program sustainability

Fiscal Architects address financial viability; however, translating sustainable models into practical, daily operations calls for a different perspective. Operational customers provide the expertise necessary to transform these financially sound solutions into seamlessly functioning realities.

How would you demonstrate ROI and financial viability to a financial customer, and what metrics would you use to validate your solution?

Operational Customer: Productivity Gurus

The middle finger represents the hand's strength and coordination, much like operational customers anchor innovation by supporting seamless implementation. These Productivity Gurus are the vital bridge between promising concepts and practical execution, safeguarding operational efficiency and integrating solutions into existing workflows.

With core customers validating the problem and financial customers assessing economic viability, operational customers concentrate on execution and implementation. While others focus on feasibility and viability, operational customers provide the expertise needed to turn potential into solutions that scale within day-to-day operations.

Their insight keeps viable innovations from stumbling during execution. Focusing on how new solutions interact with existing systems, processes, and workflows, operational customers help organizations maintain a delicate balance of productivity, efficiency, and functionality.

Understanding the Operational Customer

Operational customers bring a unique blend of systems thinking and hands-on implementation expertise. This combination allows them to engage with both the obvious and subtle aspects of workflow integration.

Their involvement begins with a meticulous evaluation of how innovations will affect existing systems. When encountering a solution, Productivity Gurus map out integration points, identify resource requirements, and propose process modifications for smooth adoption. This foresight helps them anticipate challenges that others might overlook, offering insights that bridge the gap between a solution's theoretical capabilities and its practical deployment.

Operational customers are attuned to network effects within organizations, recognizing how the value of a solution increases as more users adopt it. They also understand the coordination costs associated with scaling. For instance, they consider questions like "How will this solution function across all departments?" or "What are the training and coordination challenges when implementing across multiple shifts?" These inquiries help identify scaling difficulties early, allowing organizations to avoid missteps.

Their role is crucial, but a strong focus on system efficiency can sometimes reinforce status quo thinking. This inclination stems from a Productivity Guru's responsibility to maintain stability and their cautiousness toward disruption, often shaped by experiences with previous failed deployments. Although this caution may delay adoption, it acts as a safeguard allowing only thoroughly vetted solutions to proceed and flagging potential issues early. Their skepticism helps refine ideas, ensuring that only those with real operational benefits move forward.

Case Study: Metric Mate's Journey from Individual Users to Institutional Impact

Through conversations with MT Strickland, CEO and cofounder of Metric Mate, on November 18, 2024, I witnessed how operational insights can fundamentally reshape a company's trajectory. Initially, Metric Mate was designed to help individual gym-goers track their strength training progress, but it evolved into a transformative tool for institutional impact, driven by operational customer feedback.[24]

"Initially, we were laser-focused on the individual user," Strickland shared. "We saw ourselves solving a personal fitness tracking problem. But as gym managers started engaging with our platform, they opened our eyes to a much broader operational impact we hadn't fully anticipated."

This shift emerged through detailed feedback from gym operators, who recognized value beyond individual user benefits. Members appreciated improved workout tracking, and facility managers recognized the platform's potential to revolutionize operations. Insights into equipment usage patterns enabled a shift from reactive to predictive maintenance, while space utilization data informed optimal gym layouts. Training staff could also better monitor client progress, improving resource allocation and service delivery.

One gym manager's experience exemplified this transformation. "He showed us how he was using our platform to make facility-wide decisions," Strickland recalled. "When we were talking about individual workout tracking, he was mapping equipment utilization across the entire facility. He could finally see which machines were overcrowded, which were underutilized, and how to optimize the floor plan for better flow."

This operational perspective underscored a pivotal realization. The benefits at the individual level were clear, yet it was the institutional outcomes that proved truly transformative. Metric Mate's data empowered gym managers to make informed decisions on equipment investments, staff scheduling, and facility layout, transforming everyday fitness tracking into a driver of operational excellence.

The pivot to a B2B focus wasn't purely a strategic decision; it was a natural evolution. Operational customers revealed aggregated value that went unnoticed when viewing the product exclusively through an individual user lens. Their systematic approach to implementation and process integration uncovered opportunities that reshaped Metric Mate's direction.

Operational customer insights helped Metric Mate evolve from a personal fitness tool into a platform that drives institutional efficiency. Their expertise unlocked new opportunities for innovation that might have otherwise gone unnoticed.

[Note: This case study is based on direct interviews with MT Strickland, CEO and cofounder of Metric Mate. To learn more about MT Strickland's vision and Metric Mate's innovative approach to transforming strength training equipment, visit www.themetricmate.com.]

Operational Customer Behaviors and Expressions

The most telling behaviors of operational customers surface during initial solution demonstrations. These customers reveal their unique perspective through distinct behaviors, particularly during solution demonstrations. When they say, "Walk me through how this fits into our current workflow," they aren't merely inquiring about features. Instead, they are signaling that successful implementation depends on seamless integration with existing processes. Their immediate focus on scalability is often evident in questions like "How would this roll out across multiple departments?" or "What's the process for expanding from our pilot unit to the entire hospital?"

Their inquiries often follow a characteristic pattern, dominated by "What happens when . . ." scenarios. These questions reveal layers of operational complexity. For example, when Dr. Ugwonali introduced MedTrans Go to hospital operations managers, their first questions focused less on what the technology could do and more on how it would fit into existing workflows and systems.

» "How does this connect with our scheduling system?"
» "What happens when a patient needs multiple stops?"
» "How do we handle last-minute changes?"

Productivity Gurus also express their insights on organizational scale through statements beginning with "In our current process . . ." followed by detailed workflow descriptions. These aren't simply procedural notes; they reflect critical operational knowledge that shapes how innovations must adapt across different units or departments. This depth of understanding often leads them to provide feedback through process mapping, where they instinctively sketch diagrams to show workflow interconnections and the ripple effects of changes across the organization. Statements like "Let me show you how this would need to work" underscore their skill in mapping both immediate implementation needs and pathways for broader adoption.

Operational customers think in terms of:
» Integration with existing systems across departments
» Impact on workflows at various organizational levels
» Staff training requirements for widespread adoption
» Change management considerations for rollout
» Opportunities for process standardization to enable scaling
» Network effects as solutions spread throughout the organization

These behavioral patterns make operational customers readily identifiable. Their focus on practical implementation, system-wide impact, and organizational scaling helps innovations succeed not in isolation, but across complex organizational landscapes.

Tools and Methods for Engagement

Operational customers rely on detailed methods to evaluate and implement potential solutions. Their approach integrates systematic analysis with practical planning, creating a comprehensive framework for successful adoption. They employ project management tools such as Gantt charts, critical path analyses, and resource allocation matrices. These instruments enable operational customers to visualize and track the intricate interdependencies of implementation, from pilot programs to full-scale rollouts.

Process mapping is another critical tool, allowing operational customers to design detailed workflow diagrams that highlight both departmental processes and the broader interconnections between units. This mapping helps them anticipate how changes will ripple through the organization. They focus on key operational metrics, including throughput rates, error frequencies, waste reduction, cycle times, and quality indicators. Metrics that often become the foundation for evaluating implementation success.

Implementation planning frameworks further enhance their methodology. These frameworks combine traditional project management techniques with specialized implementation matrices to track process metrics and coordination needs, including:

- » Current state process flows and baseline performance metrics
- » System integration requirements and interface points
- » Cross-departmental coordination needs
- » Resource allocation planning
- » Training program development
- » Quality control checkpoints
- » Waste reduction targets
- » Error rate monitoring protocols

When scaling solutions, Productivity Gurus frequently utilize pilot program designs and phased implementation plans. By leveraging project management tools, they model rollout scenarios, tracking progress at both individual and cross-departmental levels. This metrics-driven approach helps identify coordination costs and bottlenecks before they hinder broader deployment.

Impact and Value Creation

In the implementation phase, Productivity Gurus become architects of integration. Their grasp of workflows and cross-departmental dynamics allows them to provide timely, relevant feedback that helps prevent costly coordination failures. Often, they design innovation-specific implementation plans that support onboarding, bridge capability gaps, and ensure solutions fit within the organization's daily operations.

For instance, one urologist I worked with developed a system to set up and tear down the robotic surgery equipment, aiming to improve throughput. The framework included standardized checklists for setup, a streamlined process for teardown, and a training protocol for the surgical team. This system significantly reduced turnover time, improved team coordination, and helped surgical staff get up to speed more quickly while maintaining surgical quality.

Operational customers' intimate knowledge of processes and systems also means they can be formidable barriers to expansion if their concerns are not addressed. When they raise issues about integration challenges, coordination costs, or process disruptions, their insights are cautionary. Ignoring these concerns can lead to failed implementations or stalled expansions. Their skepticism, though sometimes viewed as resistance, often serves as an early warning system for potential scaling problems that could undermine broader adoption.

Operational customers not only have the ability to accelerate organization-wide adoption, but they also help prevent solutions from grinding to a halt. Their everyday experience and process expertise make them trusted advocates within their professional networks. When they share implementation failures or success stories, their recommendations carry exceptional weight, as they are grounded in practical application. Below is a snapshot of the operational customer's profile.

Operational Customer Archetype Profile: The Productivity Gurus

CATEGORY	DESCRIPTION	EXAMPLE
Key Characteristics	Master of efficiency and workflow optimization. Systems thinker focused on maximizing productivity and minimizing waste. Skeptical of disruptions that might impact established workflows. Driven by metrics and performance data.	A manufacturing plant manager tracking production rates, equipment utilization, and quality metrics across assembly lines
Problem Connection	Natural efficiency expert who sees operations as interconnected systems. Views challenges through the lens of productivity enhancement and resource optimization.	Supply chain directors optimize warehouse automation systems to maximize throughput and maintain inventory accuracy
Typical Behaviors	Proactive statements like "Show me the workflow impact," "How will this affect our throughput?" and "What's our contingency plan?" Constant focus on efficiency metrics.	An airline manager analyzing how new gate scheduling technology affects aircraft turnaround times and crew utilization
Preferred Tools	Productivity dashboards, efficiency metrics, workflow analyzers, resource allocation tools, throughput tracking systems	Distribution center supervisors using real-time analytics to track order fulfillment rates and identify process bottlenecks
Value Creation	Optimizes performance through systematic analysis and continuous improvement. Drives performance through continuous improvement, streamlines onboarding, and scales team adoption.	Operations leaders in software companies who develop agile workflows that maximize developer productivity and release efficiency
Foundation Role	Like a master conductor, orchestrates complex systems to achieve peak performance. Helps innovations enhance rather than disrupt operations.	The retail manager who transforms e-commerce platforms into efficient, scalable fulfillment systems

Their commitment to implementation excellence is critical, but achieving long-term success also demands alignment with broader organizational goals and market strategies. This transition from operational execution to strategic foresight is where the role of strategic customers becomes essential. Strategic customers provide the vision and organizational influence needed to create the context in which operational excellence can truly thrive.

> *Have you had to adjust your implementation timeline to match a customer's operational rhythm or constraints? What did that require of your team?*

Strategic Customer: Visionary Trailblazers

Like the ring finger's enduring symbolism of commitment and lasting bonds, strategic customers embody an organization's dedication to transformative change. These Visionary Trailblazers possess a unique ability to see beyond immediate challenges, focusing instead on possibilities that create competitive advantages.

Unlike operational customers, who emphasize efficiency, or financial customers, who prioritize economic returns, strategic customers play a longer game. They seek innovations capable of fundamentally altering their competitive position, creating new market opportunities, or reshaping their industry. Occupying roles where they influence organizational direction, their true power lies in envisioning and championing transformative change.

Understanding strategic customers is essential for innovators because these individuals often serve as catalysts for large-scale adoption. Their support accelerates market acceptance, provides access to resources, and generates the organizational momentum needed for successful innovation implementation. Strategic customers seek solutions that align with their long-term vision and deliver a competitive edge.

Understanding the Strategic Customer

Strategic customers distinguish themselves by their willingness to pursue breakthrough innovations that reshape market dynamics. Unlike other customer types, they are motivated by the potential to create competitive advantages and seize new market opportunities.

What sets strategic customers apart is their focus on future possibilities rather than current limitations. When evaluating innovations, they ask questions such as "How could this reshape our industry?" or "What new opportunities might this create?" Their forward-thinking perspective drives them to champion initiatives others might deem too ambitious or uncertain.

Strategic customers influence which innovative paths the organization will pursue and the extent of commitment to emerging opportunities. Visionary Trailblazers assess long-term market evolution, identify competitive advantages, and consider ecosystem impacts and partnership opportunities to guide strategic initiatives.

Strategic customers balance breakthrough potential with strategic fit, guiding innovations toward alignment with long-term goals. They evaluate factors such as transformation potential, readiness for change, and emerging trends, making their perspective crucial for aligning solutions with broader market opportunities.

Case Study: Pioneering Excellence in Robotic Surgery

In 2006, I had the privilege of working with hospitals to implement robotic surgery programs, where I encountered many remarkable physicians. Among them was Dr. Feuer from Atlanta, Georgia, whose dedication to innovation and patient care stood out. Despite his strong foundation in traditional open surgery, Dr. Feuer recognized the growing importance of minimally invasive techniques and the transformative potential of robotic surgery. His willingness to embrace this emerging technology reflected his forward-thinking approach to advancing medical care.[25]

In our discussions about the future of surgical procedures, Dr. Feuer expressed his ambition to lead the way in robotic surgery. With confident declarations such as "We will be the first" and "We want to be the market leader," he exemplified the visionary boldness that defines a strategic customer. His determination to pioneer new advancements was evident, and his enthusiasm for robotic surgery underscored his commitment to staying ahead of industry trends.

Dr. Feuer's vision extended beyond clinical benefits. He anticipated how robotic surgery could revolutionize his patient care, offering unparalleled precision and outcomes while meeting the growing demand for less-invasive options. "Is anyone else using this?" he once exclaimed, underscoring his drive to distinguish himself as an innovator in his field. He understood that adopting robotic surgery early would not only elevate patient care but also secure his practice's competitive edge in an evolving healthcare landscape.

This visionary approach was matched by Dr. Feuer's practical actions.

He was instrumental in starting multiple robotic surgery programs and training hundreds of surgeons worldwide in robotic gynecologic oncology procedures. With more than six thousand robotic cases performed, Dr. Feuer has established himself as one of the foremost robotic surgeons globally. A testament to his relentless pursuit of excellence and innovation.

Dr. Feuer's expertise became profoundly personal for me when he later performed robotic surgery on my wife. Witnessing firsthand the precision and care he brought to the procedure reinforced the life-changing potential of his work. His pioneering contributions have transformed not only his practice but countless lives, setting a new standard in surgical care.

Tools and Methods for Engagement

Strategic customers evaluate potential innovations using a blend of established strategic frameworks, such as Blue Ocean Strategy and Porter's Five Forces, with a strong emphasis on competitive positioning and market transformation. Their evaluation combines high-level strategic analysis with practical market assessments. They seek metrics that demonstrate leadership in innovation, quality, and market share, viewing these as signs of sustained organizational success.

Strategic planning tools are central to their approach. Visionary Trailblazers rely on frameworks such as competitive analysis, market positioning maps, and strategic road maps to evaluate how innovations might influence industry dynamics.

Engaging stakeholders is also a key part of their process. They often organize cross-functional leadership teams to assess innovations from multiple strategic perspectives, which include:
- » Executive leadership roundtables
- » Strategic planning workshops
- » Competitive positioning analyses
- » Market opportunity assessments
- » Innovation road map development
- » Strategic partnership evaluations

Their approach also incorporates scenario planning, helping them envision different market evolutions and assess how various strategies will affect competitive dynamics.

Impact and Value Creation

Visionary Trailblazers influence extends far beyond individual purchase decisions, significantly altering how organizations position themselves within evolving market landscapes. In the early stages of adoption, strategic customers serve as visionary champions who recognize the transformative potential of new solutions. When they collaborate with core customers who bring critical problem expertise, they help accelerate the path from concept to market leadership. This synergy between strategic vision and practical insight speeds up decision-making and implementation.

Core customers bring urgency rooted in solving pressing problems. Strategic customers feel urgency around seizing market advantage. When these perspectives align, innovation gains both traction and momentum, grounded in real need and propelled by opportunity.

Strategic customers create value by shaping industry standards and establishing barriers to competition through early adoption. They build innovation ecosystems through strategic partnerships and collaborations, accelerating market development and solidifying their position as market leaders. Their influence not only impacts their own organizations but also drives broader industry evolution.

Strategic customers reinvest in technologies that deliver real strategic advantage. These reinvestments do more than expand adoption. They send a clear signal to both internal and external stakeholders that the innovation is producing results. Each new phase of implementation creates opportunities to refine processes, reduce costs, and improve overall performance. Over time, these outcomes strengthen the innovation's strategic value and solidify its role in the organization's market position. This visible progress shapes how others in the industry perceive the solution, lowers the sense of risk, and often sets the stage for broader market acceptances.

Strategic Customer Archetype Profile: Visionary Trailblazers

As the table below illustrates, these customers are highly attuned to industry trends, competitive threats, and growth opportunities, enabling them to foresee the future and shape their organization's trajectory accordingly.

CATEGORY	DESCRIPTION	EXAMPLE
Key Characteristics	Market-focused leader who prioritizes competitive positioning and long-term organizational success. Highly attuned to industry trends, competitive threats, and growth opportunities.	A healthcare CEO evaluating market position against competing health systems
Problem Connection	Views challenges through the lens of competitive advantage and market leadership. Focuses on threats to market position and opportunities for differentiation.	An airline executive evaluating international route expansion
Typical Behaviors	Asks questions about competitive position, market share, and the long-term impact. Constantly scanning the competitive landscape.	A luxury brand president assessing emerging consumer lifestyle trends
Preferred Tools	Market analysis reports, competitive intelligence dashboards, strategic planning frameworks (Porter's Five Forces, Blue Ocean Strategy), scenario planning tools	A social media platform strategist using engagement analytic tools
Value Creation	Creates sustainable competitive advantages through market positioning, strategic partnerships, and organizational capabilities	Consumer brand executives building direct-to-consumer channels
Foundation Role	Acts as a strategic architect, designing and implementing initiatives that secure long-term market leadership positions	A food and beverage executive revolutionizing personalized nutrition

Understanding and effectively engaging strategic customers is vital for innovators seeking to align their solutions with future market trends and create lasting impact. Fostering partnerships with these visionary leaders unlocks the full potential of innovation and drives transformative change across industries.

Have you encountered customers who made decisions with long-term competitive advantage in mind? How did they influence the direction of your solution?

Social Customer: Network Ambassadors

As noted earlier, the pinky finger contributes up to 50 percent of the hand's overall grip strength, despite its smaller size. This serves as a metaphor for the often underestimated yet crucial role of social customers in driving innovation adoption. These community-focused champions prioritize social responsibility over traditional success metrics, evaluating solutions based on their potential to drive societal benefits.

Social customers represent an archetype that seeks the intersection of innovation and social good. Their focus transcends individual or organizational gains, concentrating instead on how innovations address broader societal challenges and promote inclusive growth and sustainable development.

Other customer types may evaluate solutions based on functionality or financial returns; Network Ambassadors, however, assess innovations through their potential to:

» Create positive community impact
» Build sustainable support networks
» Drive collective benefit

Rather than being passive observers, social customers are active participants, closely connected to the communities they serve.

Understanding the Social Customer

Social customers evaluate innovations through a distinctive lens that prioritizes community well-being and collective progress. They assess value based on how innovations create positive impacts across diverse community groups.

Their evaluation criteria differ from traditional metrics, emphasizing accessibility, equity, and long-term societal benefits. When considering potential innovations, they ask questions such as:

» How will this benefit different segments of our community?
» What are the broader implications for society's most vulnerable members?

Network Ambassadors demonstrate their focus through active involvement in grassroots organizations, civic initiatives, and advocacy efforts. They excel at bridging gaps between stakeholders, fostering collaboration, and documenting the societal impacts of new solutions. Their advocacy is rooted in the belief that progress should uplift entire communities, not a privileged few.

Their value lies in their insight into creating opportunities that drive meaningful social impact. By understanding community dynamics and societal needs, they evaluate how innovations affect different population segments. They identify adoption barriers, offer insights into community acceptance, and provide feedback to help align solutions with societal priorities.

In the broader context of innovation adoption, social customers serve as guardians of community interests, guiding progress to reflect societal values. By prioritizing fairness, accessibility, and long-term benefits, they help organizations balance technological progress with social responsibility, fostering more sustainable growth across society.

Case Study: RICE—Innovation Through Community Impact

The Russell Innovation Center for Entrepreneurs (RICE) in Atlanta exemplifies how social customers drive innovation with a community-centered approach.[26] Founded in the spirit of legendary Atlanta entrepreneur Herman J. Russell, whose legacy of economic empowerment and civic leadership laid the groundwork for inclusive entrepreneurship, RICE continues to build on his vision of transformative community impact.

With more than 400 stakeholders RICE has created an ecosystem that transforms individual entrepreneurial success into collective community advancement. Jay Bailey, RICE's leader, embodies the social customer archetype. When RICE opened its doors in 2019, Bailey recognized a pressing issue. Despite Atlanta's high number of Black entrepreneurs, only 4 percent of Black-owned businesses survive the startup stage. He saw entrepreneurship support not as a service, but as a catalyst for societal transformation, addressing the barriers Black entrepreneurs face.

RICE's approach incorporates its Six C's framework—community, connections, curriculum, capital, coaching, and culture. Every initiative is assessed through the lens of collective benefit, with stakeholder input directly influencing program development. Success is tracked through metrics like engagement, utilization, collaborations, and revenues from RICE-affiliated businesses.

RICE's success offers compelling evidence of its model in action. Forty-six percent of RICE entrepreneurs thrive beyond the startup stage, which is ten times the national average, and since 2020, RICE-affiliated businesses have created 1,318 new jobs. The center achieved $19.5 million in direct spending with Black-owned businesses and reached 10,000 entrepreneurs through its programs in 2022.[27]

RICE's commitment to fostering a flourishing ecosystem for Black entrepreneurs is evident in its comprehensive programs. Initiatives like the Big IDEAS Learning Platform and Digital RICE provide resources and mentorship. The Level UP Speaker Series and Data Science Initiative offer valuable guidance in critical business areas.

RICE's example illustrates how social customers drive innovation through solutions that create meaningful change. Their approach shows that successful innovation is not just about introducing new ideas. It makes a positive difference tackling the barriers that hold communities back.

[Note: To learn more about the Russell Innovation Center for Entrepreneurs and their impactful work, visit www.RussellCenter.org. RICE welcomes thousands of visitors monthly and hosts more than twenty-five community events per week, making it the nation's largest nonprofit center focused exclusively on Black entrepreneurs.]

Social Customer Behaviors and Expressions

Social customers begin discussions about potential solutions with a focus on community impact. For example, when American Heart Association representatives ask how an idea will improve heart health across diverse groups, they are focused not only on individual outcomes but on creating positive change for entire communities.

Their questions reflect a grounded awareness of the challenges communities face. When RICE leadership says, "We need solutions that support Black entrepreneurs and boost economic empowerment in underserved areas," they speak from lived experience and deep engagement with community dynamics. These statements move past procedural details to consider how innovations influence broader segments of the community.

For Network Ambassadors, success is about what changes for the broader community. Instead of focusing on the functionality or financial outcomes of a solution, they ask, "What happens when . . ." questions that highlight the long-term societal effects. For instance, when Red Cross representatives ask what a decision will mean for communities hit by disasters, they are offering crucial perspectives that assess the social viability of a solution, informed by both successful and failed community initiatives.

Organizations like Goodie Nation[28] and ATDC[29] consistently evaluate innovations with a focus on broader societal benefit. When Goodie Nation advocates say, "We should focus on projects that promote fairness." This reflects a core trait of social customers who connect individual initiatives to broader social change. Similarly, ATDC's work with tech startups in Georgia demonstrates how social customers help innovations make a meaningful difference across technical founder communities.

These behaviors help distinguish social customers from other archetypes. Core customers focus on solving specific problems, financial customers emphasize economic returns, and social customers prioritize community-wide or aggregated impact.

Tools and Methods for Engagement

Network Ambassadors employ distinctive methods to evaluate and engage with potential solutions. Their approach combines grassroots engagement with structured analysis to assess social impact.

Community engagement platforms are their primary tools. For example, when the American Heart Association evaluates new health initiatives, they rely on focus groups, community forums, and stakeholder workshops to gather feedback from affected populations. These platforms make space for marginalized voices, offering essential insights into the impact of innovations across diverse communities.

Another vital tool is impact assessment frameworks. RICE, ATDC, and Goodie Nation create detailed analyses that focus on long-term outcomes for the communities they serve. Social customers pay particular attention to metrics such as:

- » Community economic impact
- » Access and inclusion measures
- » Stakeholder engagement levels
- » Social return on investment (SROI)
- » Long-term sustainability indicators

Storytelling and narrative collection are also powerful evaluation methods. For instance, the Red Cross gathers testimonials to understand how solutions affect real people during crises. These narratives offer essential data points that capture the human dimension of the work.

When conducting detailed analyses, social customers use personal methods, such as organizing community feedback sessions, establishing advisory boards, and using participatory action research to involve community members directly in solution development. They also use social media listening tools to capture real-time feedback and emerging community needs while conducting community needs assessments to better understand the challenges and priorities of the communities they serve. These tools and methods help social customers engage with community perspectives, leading to solutions that create meaningful change.

Impact and Value Creation

In the early adoption phase, Network Ambassadors act as more than community representatives. Their commitment to community well-being guides the development of solutions that are effective, culturally appropriate, and accessible. For example, the American Heart Association works to adapt health innovations for broader community access, extending their relevance beyond clinical settings.

Social customers' efforts in validating social contributions are crucial. As demonstrated by RICE and Goodie Nation, social customers connect bold ideas with tangible community results. With insight into community dynamics, they drive refinements that target root causes instead of surface-level issues. The Red Cross, for instance, evaluates disaster response solutions based on long-term community resilience rather than solely on immediate aid.

Social Customer Archetype Profile: Network Ambassadors

Social customers' strong connection to community needs enable organizations to align technological advancements with meaningful social change. Through organizations like the National Veteran-Owned Business Association supporting veteran entrepreneurs,[30] RICE empowering Black business owners, and Thrive Farmers creating sustainable agricultural communities,[31] social customers demonstrate how focused advocacy can transform innovations into vehicles for community empowerment.

The table below illustrates how these customers help guide organizations in aligning innovations with societal needs, making sure progress benefits everyone, particularly marginalized communities.

CATEGORY	DESCRIPTION	EXAMPLE
Key Characteristics	Deep understanding of community needs. Strong commitment to social justice and equity. Skeptical of solutions that overlook community needs and consequences. Personal investment in community well-being.	RICE supporting Black entrepreneurs by focusing on solutions that promote economic empowerment and sustainable growth
Problem Connection	Combines community expertise with emotional investment in social impact. Views challenges through the lens of community benefit and collective well-being.	The National Veteran-Owned Business Association's dedication to creating corporate contracting opportunities for veteran-owned businesses
Typical Behaviors	Proactive questions about benefits for their community, accessibility, and considering all stakeholders. Active engagement in community consultation.	ATDC's community catalysts providing resources designed to meet their community's needs
Preferred Tools	Community feedback sessions, stakeholder surveys, impact assessments, social media listening tools, participatory research methods.	Goodie Nation's use of community feedback sessions and impact measurement tools to evaluate startup solutions' social impact
Value Creation	Contributes more than advocacy through community-rooted insights, real-world validation, and authentic engagement.	Thrive Farmers' creation of sustainable income models for coffee farmers
Foundation Role	Serving as a bridge between innovation and community, this role provides a vital connection that helps solutions create real social value. It reflects a strong commitment to community benefit and equitable access.	The Local Initiatives Support Corporation connecting local groups with resources to tackle community challenges and drive sustainable development

Have you worked with customers who prioritized broader community benefit or social good in their decision-making? How did that shape your approach?

CFOSS Customer Overview

To recap the CFOSS customer archetypes, below is a table that provides an overview of each customer type's key characteristics, primary focus, typical behaviors, and value creation. This comprehensive summary helps organizations understand the diverse stakeholders they engage with and tailor their strategies to meet their specific needs and objectives.

Customer Type	Key Characteristics	Primary Focus	Typical Behaviors	Value Creation
Core	Expertise in the problem space; persistent problem-solving mindset; skeptical yet open to innovation; personal investment in outcomes	Direct problem resolution	"Let me try it," active solution testing, detailed feedback, hands-on experimentation	Provides crucial insights and validation
Financial	ROI-driven perspective; risk-aware mindset; data-focused analysis; resource optimization	Economic value	Cost-benefit analysis, financial modeling, risk assessment, budget alignment	Ensures financial viability and sustainable growth.
Operational	System-level thinking; process optimization focus; integration expertise; efficiency-driven	Seamless implementation and scaling	Workflow analysis, integration planning, process improvement, system optimization	Enables successful deployment and scaling
Strategic	Long-term vision; competitive advantage focus; market-oriented thinking; innovation-driven	Organizational advancement	Market analysis, competitive positioning, strategic alignment, future planning	Drives organizational growth and innovation
Social	Deep understanding of community needs; strong commitment to social justice and equity; skeptical of solutions that don't consider community impact; personal investment in community well-being	Societal value creation	Community engagement, impact assessment, stakeholder advocacy, inclusive solution design	Promotes meaningful social impact and sustainable adoption

Navigating Customer Complexities

Understanding the complexities of customer needs requires recognizing that these needs are often interrelated and multifaceted. Consider three critical aspects of customer engagement: the interconnected nature of CFOSS customer needs, the reality of multiple priorities within a single customer, and the dynamic relationships between B2B stakeholders. Each of these areas plays a pivotal role in understanding customers' diverse range of demands.

The Interconnected Nature of CFOSS Customer Needs

We've explored each CFOSS customer archetype individually, but it's important to recognize that these needs rarely exist in isolation. Like the coordinated movement of fingers forming a strong grip, CFOSS customer needs are intricately interwoven. A web of priorities and considerations that must be addressed holistically.

Consider the infection preventionist from our earlier case study. Her primary motivation reflected core customer traits, grounded in a strong desire to understand and solve the HAI problem. At the same time, she also evaluated:

» Financial implications of new solutions (financial)
» Integration with existing hospital protocols (operational)
» Long-term effect on hospital reputation (strategic)
» Community health outcomes (social)

Multiple Priorities, One Customer

In practice, individuals often embody multiple CFOSS archetypes simultaneously. A hospital CFO, for example, might primarily focus on financial considerations but also have strong concerns about operational efficiency and strategic positioning. This multi-dimensional nature of customer needs is a hallmark of decision-making and highlights the complexity involved in evaluating innovations.

The B2B Stakeholder Dynamic

In B2B settings, the complexity of decision-making is further amplified as stakeholders within the same organization embody varied CFOSS archetypes. For instance:

» Clinical directors, deeply invested in solving problems, naturally align with core characteristics as they seek solutions to improve patient care.
» Finance teams, focused on ROI and cost savings, embody the

financial archetype's concern with economic viability.

» IT departments, tasked with system integration and workflow optimization, represent the operational perspective and support the alignment of new solutions with existing processes.

» At the executive level, C-suite leaders evaluate opportunities through a strategic lens, considering long-term competitive positioning and market leadership.

» Community relations teams bring the social perspective, assessing how innovations influence broader stakeholder relationships and community well-being.

However, as illustrated by the da Vinci Surgical System example in chapter 2, successful adoption requires addressing all these interconnected needs cohesively. The system achieved success not only by solving challenges associated with transitioning from open procedures to minimally invasive surgery (core) but also by delivering measurable financial benefits, operational efficiencies, strategic advantages, and positive social impacts. For a deeper exploration of how these customer archetypes function in practice, refer to Appendix A, which examines robotic surgery customer archetypes from 1999–2004 as a detailed case study. This example underscores that effective innovation engages all CFOSS dimensions to earn broad organizational support and drive successful adoption.

The interconnected nature of CFOSS customer needs emphasizes why successful innovation adoption requires multi-dimensional value propositions. As we move into Chapter 4, we'll explore how to craft value propositions that address the full spectrum of CFOSS customer needs, creating compelling narratives that reflect what matters most to each stakeholder.

CHAPTER 3 IN REVIEW

Understanding CFOSS Customer Archetypes

- » CFOSS customer archetypes play distinct yet interconnected roles in the innovation adoption process.
- » Core customers (Problem Pioneers) focus on solving specific problems, offering deep insights and hands-on testing.
- » Financial customers (Fiscal Architects) prioritize economic sustainability and ROI, evaluating innovations based on long-term financial viability.
- » Operational customers (Productivity Gurus) emphasize efficient integration and scalable solutions to support smooth implementation across systems.
- » Strategic customers (Visionary Trailblazers) focus on long-term market positioning and competitive advantage, often driving the direction of organizational transformation.
- » Social customers (Network Ambassadors) advocate for community impact, focusing on social responsibility and helping innovations address broader societal challenges.
- » CFOSS customer needs are interconnected. A customer may prioritize more than one archetype simultaneously, and their needs evolve as the innovation progresses.

Scan to watch the Chapter Overview Video.
Get a quick summary, key insights, and what to look for in the upcoming chapter.

CHAPTER 04

To put everything in balance is good, to put everything in harmony is better.
—Victor Hugo

Unveiling the Layers of CFOSS® Value

The journey from innovation to adoption demands creating value that resonates across customer needs. Value propositions act as the bridge between your solution and customer expectations, addressing their challenges and desires. These propositions, much like the innovations they represent, are dynamic and evolve with changing customer priorities and market conditions.

While traditional value propositions often emphasize features or single-dimension benefits, the CFOSS framework offers a multidimensional approach to value creation. Each CFOSS pillar contributes to crafting value propositions that address the unique needs of diverse customer types and organizational priorities.

This chapter lays the groundwork for creating CFOSS aligned value propositions. Mastering this approach will help you:
- » Differentiate your innovation in competitive markets
- » Attract and engage the right customers
- » Address diverse stakeholder needs to accelerate adoption
- » Build sustainable competitive advantages
- » Deliver value across CFOSS dimensions

Let's begin by exploring how CFOSS builds on scholarly insights and emphasizes how businesses create value through meeting the multifaceted needs of their customers.

Building on Scholarly Insights

Understanding the theoretical foundations of value creation is essential to fully grasp the relevance and power of the CFOSS framework. While many adoption models emphasize timing or categories of adopters, the scholars below have helped shift the conversation toward a richer understanding of how value is perceived, created, and exchanged. CFOSS builds on these insights.

Jay B. Barney emphasized that value propositions must highlight uniqueness and differentiation, stressing the importance of standing out from competitors.[32] This concept is illustrated by Apple's approach in the smartphone market. Other companies offered similar technology, but Apple's emphasis on unique design, user experience, and ecosystem integration established a strong market position and cultivated brand loyalty.

Richard Normann and Rafael Ramirez introduced the concept of value co-creation, showing that value isn't just delivered by companies to passive customers. It's created collaboratively with customers, partners, and even competitors.[33] Lego's customer-driven innovation model is a powerful example. Lego invited fans to contribute ideas for new sets and rewarded the most popular ones. This approach created better-aligned products and strengthened customer engagement.

Christian Grönroos and Stanley F. Slater highlighted the role of customer relationships in creating value, showing that value emerges from ongoing interactions.[34] Starbucks exemplifies this through its rewards program, which creates personalized experiences for customers. By continually engaging with consumers, Starbucks fosters loyalty and generates long-term value that extends beyond the coffee itself.

Michael Porter's value chain framework stressed the interconnectedness of value creation across activities, with later scholars like Ajay Menon and Christian Homburg focusing on differentiation at every stage.[35] Southwest Airlines provides a strong example of this. The company integrates customer service, a low-cost structure, and quick turnaround times into a seamless value chain that delivers exceptional service and sustains cost leadership.

Lastly, Clayton Christensen redefined value propositions with his Jobs to Be Done framework, shifting the focus from features to the functional, emotional, and social needs customers aim to fulfill.[36] Netflix's transition from DVD rentals to streaming demonstrates this shift. The company offered more than movies. It tapped into the customer desire for instant access to entertainment, fulfilling both convenience and social connection needs in a way that traditional video rental services could not.

While these theories provide foundational insights, traditional definitions of value propositions often fall short. Eric Ries describes a value proposition as "the reason someone should choose your product over competitors,"[37] but this view may ignore the customer complexities. Similarly, Osterwalder's Business Model Canvas is frequently applied with a focus on single-segment value creation,[38] overlooking the complexity of multifaceted customer needs.

This is where CFOSS offers a transformative approach. By building on these scholarly insights, CFOSS integrates five critical pillars. In the upcoming sections, we will break down each value proposition through the following structure:

1. The Foundation and Key Principles: How each value proposition is built upon a CFOSS understanding of customer needs and motivations.

2. Value Proposition in Action: How leading organizations implement these propositions in real-world scenarios.

3. Alignment: Why aligning value propositions with customer priorities is crucial for success across all CFOSS dimensions.

4. Crafting Value Propositions: A step-by-step approach to designing and communicating offerings that speak directly to the needs and priorities of each customer archetype.

5. Why Alignment Matters: How proper alignment accelerates adop-

tion, drives growth, and fosters long-term loyalty.

Core Value Propositions: The Foundation of Value Creation

The Core Value Proposition (CVP) represents the core purpose and primary value of your offering. CVPs are the driving force within the CFOSS framework, representing the heart of an organization's mission, vision, and purpose. Where the Core Pillar addresses the 'why' of an organization, the CVP defines the 'what's in it for me' from the customer's perspective. The CVP presents customers with a compelling reason to engage with the offering.

Like the nucleus of a cell directing all its functions, the CVP influences every aspect of an organization's value creation process, from operations to customer engagement. It's more than a tagline or slogan. It represents the why behind the organization's existence, driving alignment across all CFOSS dimensions.

Core Value in Action: Learning from Market Leaders

The practical application of CVPs can be seen in the strategies of market leaders like Chick-fil-A, Starbucks, and Intuitive Surgical. These organizations show how a well-crafted CVP can strongly appeal to core customers, driving adoption.

Chick-fil-A's CVP centers on providing high-quality, freshly prepared food paired with exceptional customer service. This value proposition goes beyond food quality, creating a personalized experience. Chick-fil-A consistently delivers on its promise through employee training, where staff members are empowered to anticipate customer needs, turning routine dining into memorable experiences. This reflects the core value of delivering consistent and outstanding service, resonating with customers seeking both quality and human connection.

Starbucks transformed the simple act of drinking coffee into a premium experience. Their CVP centers not just on coffee but on creating an atmosphere of community and connection. Baristas are trained to deliver an extraordinary customer experience, and digital tools like mobile ordering and rewards programs further enhance the value proposition. Starbucks created a compelling offering that appeals to both the functional needs of the customer (good coffee) and their emotional needs (a place to relax, connect, and feel part of something bigger).

Initially, the da Vinci system's CVP was focused on enabling minimally invasive surgery for procedures that were traditionally performed using open techniques. This supported core healthcare needs through improved patient outcomes, including reduced scarring, pain, and recovery time.[39] Over time, the CVP evolved as laparoscopic surgeons adopted the technology and began refining its use for their specific needs. The da Vinci system's CVP is an example of how a company's value proposition must remain adaptable to meet evolving market demands and customer feedback.

These examples highlight the importance of crafting CVPs that connect with customer needs and evolve across different contexts. The table below summarizes how effective CVPs manifest across industries.

Value Prop.	Definition	Chick-fil-A	Starbucks	Robotic Surgery: 1999-2004
Core	The primary benefit(s) a product or service provides, defining its essence and compelling customers to choose it	High-quality, freshly prepared food with exceptional service	Premium beverages in community-oriented spaces	Enabling minimally invasive surgery for procedures traditionally performed through open techniques

Aligning Core Value Propositions with Core Customers

When the CVP fits the needs of core customers, it creates harmony that drives engagement, speeds up adoption, and builds lasting commitment. But when there's a mismatch, the result is friction that slows progress and blocks innovation from moving forward.

As we learned from Clayton Christensen's Jobs to Be Done framework, customers don't simply buy products. They "hire" them to accomplish specific objectives. Core customers are more than users of solutions. They are partners in problem-solving.

Crafting CVPs for core customers means reflecting and amplifying their priorities. This strengthens the connection between your innovation and their professional missions, positioning them as champions of adoption.

Crafting Value Propositions for Core Customers

This structured three-step process helps you craft CVPs that capture the interest and commitment of core customers.

Step 1: Understand and Reflect the Problem Connection

Core customers are deeply familiar with the complexities of the problems your solution addresses. To build trust and establish credibility, your CVP must reflect their level of understanding and expertise. For example, Tesla's core customers were passionate about sustainability and performance. They also faced practical hurdles with electric vehicle adoption, including limited range, sparse charging infrastructure, and the unfamiliarity of new technology.

Tesla's CVP offered a compelling response to customer concerns while tapping into their vision for environmental progress. The result was a solution that felt personal, purposeful, and forward-looking. When you reflect what matters most to core customers, your offering becomes more than a product. It becomes part of their mission.

Step 2: Highlight the Solution Impact

Core customers look for solutions that rethink how problems are addressed. A strong CVP should show how your offering creates clear improvements and addresses the issue from multiple angles.

Take, for instance, Amazon. Their CVP has evolved to emphasize not only a seamless shopping experience, fast delivery, and convenience for their e-commerce retail customers but also personalized services like tailored recommendations and easy returns. For core customers, Amazon's CVP reflects a broader commitment to redefining convenience, personalization, and overall value, transforming the entire customer experience.[40] Whether through innovations like Amazon Prime or Alexa, Amazon shapes its CVP around customers' needs for efficiency, immediacy, and tailored experiences.

Step 3: Align with the Customer's Professional Mission

Core customers often view problem-solving as integral to their professional identity. For your CVP to resonate, it must align with their broader mission and values. The value lies not only in the functional benefits of a solution but also in how it supports both professional and personal aspirations.

Consider Starbucks's "third place" concept. Starbucks appeals to customers who seek more than coffee. They want a place to connect, relax, and feel part of a community. The brand meets a human need for belonging and connection. Similarly, Amazon's CVP reflects customers' desire for efficiency and immediacy, seen in the ease of services like Prime and one-click ordering.

Remember, for Problem Pioneers, innovations aren't merely tools. They're extensions of their identity, enabling them to show up in the world more authentically.

After defining a strong CVP, the focus shifts to weaving it consistently into every customer interaction. For a detailed look at how the da Vinci Surgical System applied this process step by step, see Appendix B.

Achieving Alignment: Why It Matters

A strong connection between CVPs and core customers forms the foundation for customer traction. It leads to:

» **Targeted Innovation:** Solutions address specific challenges, fostering a strong product-market fit.
» **Enhanced Loyalty:** Customers feel valued and engaged, becoming advocates for your innovation.
» **Differentiation:** Tailored offerings create competitive advantages in the market.
» **Accelerated Adoption:** Resonant propositions reduce barriers to entry and encourage quicker adoption.
» **Sustainable Growth:** Loyal customers fuel long-term success through repeat engagement and valuable insights.

Core alignment initiates the process, but its impact radiates throughout your business. Mastering this critical step unlocks the potential to harmonize all CFOSS dimensions, transforming your innovation into a catalyst for success for both your customers and your organization.

Authentic connections with Problem Pioneers stem from shared purpose, while financial customers respond to a more financially grounded approach. Let's explore how aligning with Fiscal Architects transforms an innovation from an idea into an investment.

Maximizing Financial Value: Unlocking Economic Benefits

Financial Value Propositions (FVPs) serve as the bridge between innovation and economic justification. They address customers' financial concerns by focusing on cost, revenue, profitability, and long-term financial sustainability. While CVPs reflect an offering's fundamental purpose, FVPs provide the numerical evidence and rationale that validate its worth.

Remember, financial customers are analytical decision-makers who assess innovations through a precise economic lens. They seek clear answers to critical questions: How does this offering impact my financial health? What is the total cost of ownership (TCO)? What ROI can I expect and in what time frame? For these customers, purchasing a solution is less about the features and more about its ability to generate tangible, measurable financial outcomes. As such, trust hinges on a value proposition that not only outlines benefits but also mitigates risks and provides predictability.

FVPs must strike a delicate balance between immediate savings and long-term financial impact. Whether focusing on cost reductions, revenue growth, or profitability improvements, FVPs need to deliver clear, quantifiable value.

Financial Value in Action: Learning from Market Leaders

Market leaders stand out by crafting FVPs that highlight tangible financial value, earning customer confidence and buy-in.

Amazon Prime is a masterclass in crafting FVPs.[41] The membership program includes perks like expedited shipping. Financial customers also benefit from savings on shipping costs, and discounted membership tiers for students and those receiving government assistance.[42] These savings carry weight for budget-conscious consumers.

Chick-fil-A creates financial value by offering competitive pricing without compromising quality. Value meal bundles deliver an affordable yet premium dining experience. The Chick-fil-A One rewards program incentivizes repeat visits.[43]

Starbucks provides a tiered approach to financial value, accommodating diverse budgets and preserving its upscale brand identity. Customers can choose between affordable brewed coffee and premium handcrafted beverages. The Starbucks Rewards program enhances financial value by allowing customers to earn points redeemable for discounts, free items, and exclusive offers.

Initially, the da Vinci Surgical System's FVP centered on reducing costs associated with open surgery. By enabling minimally invasive techniques, it promised shorter hospital stays, fewer complications, and lower overall treatment costs.[44] These benefits appealed to hospitals focused on operational efficiency and cost containment. As adoption grew, the financial narrative expanded to include benefits like enhanced patient throughput and competitive differentiation.

Value Prop.	Definition	Chick-fil-A	Starbucks	Robotic Surgery: 1999-2004
Financial	How an innovation impacts a customer's financial landscape, including cost, revenue, and profitability	Competitive pricing, value meal options, and rewards program (Chick-fil-A One)	Tiered pricing and Starbucks Rewards for discounts and perks	Lower treatment costs, reduced hospital stays, and other savings for healthcare providers

Seen by these examples, FVPs emphasize clear economic benefits, adaptability to varied customer needs, and a sustained focus on long-term financial advantages. In doing so, these companies help customers perceive their offerings not as expenses but as strategic investments.

Aligning Financial Value Propositions with Financial Customers

Financial customers, such as CFOs, budget directors, and financial analysts, rely on data-driven narratives that emphasize profitability, risk mitigation, and ROI. For these decision-makers, without financial clarity, even the most innovative solutions struggle to gain traction.

When your offering speaks directly to financial metrics and priorities, it transitions from being perceived as an expense to being recognized as an asset.

Crafting Value Propositions for Financial Customers

Creating effective FVPs begins with understanding the unique mindset and priorities of Fiscal Architects. Financial customers evaluate solutions through a fiscal lens. They weigh the potential for value creation against financial risks and demand evidence of measurable economic outcomes.

The process of crafting compelling FVPs involves three key steps:

Step 1: Define the Economic Impact

Financial customers require a clear understanding of how your solution affects their organization's financial health. This includes demonstrating cost savings, revenue enhancements, and overall ROI. To meet this need, articulate how your offering will affect resource allocation, operational budgets, and organizational profitability. For example, a cloud software provider might highlight how its platform reduces up-front IT costs and ongoing maintenance expenses.

Step 2: Present a Clear Risk-Return Analysis

Financial customers are stewards of organizational resources, and their decisions hinge on a thorough understanding of risk and return. Your FVP must present a balanced perspective that outlines potential benefits alongside possible risks, coupled with clear strategies for mitigating those risks. For instance, a renewable energy provider might emphasize performance guarantees or insurance-backed assurances to reduce perceived risks, and highlight how reduced energy costs offer immediate financial relief.

The risk in this context is that your current offering may not yield strong financial value in the short term, especially if it fails to meet specific market or customer demands. This risk is crucial to identify early, as it influences both your positioning and how you address the financial concerns of your customers.

Step 3: Validate Scalability and Long-Term Viability

Financial customers often evaluate innovations with an eye on scalability. Discuss how your offering's financial benefits evolve over time. Highlight potential cost efficiencies, revenue enhancements, or margin improvements that scale with broader implementation. For instance, a logistics tech firm might demonstrate how increased shipment volume leads to lower per-unit costs.

Demonstrating that you understand the perspective of the financial customer and can back it up with data and evidence is key to earning their trust.

What specific economic metrics do financial customers use to evaluate your solution? How can you further validate its financial impact to enhance credibility?

A strong FVP today may lose its impact tomorrow if it fails to evolve with market changes, competitor innovations, or shifting customer priorities. This is why continuous monitoring and adaptation are crucial. For a deeper exploration of this dynamic, refer to the robotic surgery example in Appendix B.

Achieving Alignment: Why It Matters

Remember, value propositions transform your offering from an expense into a strategic asset. Financial alignment results in:

- » Credibility Through Economic Insight: Financial decision-makers demand tangible data demonstrating measurable financial returns.
- » Streamlined Decision-Making: Precise, relevant financial benefits simplify decision-making for financial leaders.
- » Risk Mitigation and Confidence Building: Demonstrating predictable returns and minimizing exposure to potential losses reassures financial customers and encourages adoption.
- » Foundations for Long-Term Growth: Consistent financial performance fosters enduring relationships, driving renewal, investment expansion, and collaboration opportunities.
- » Scalable Pricing Strategies: Tailored pricing models that reflect economic value help keep your offering relevant and adaptable to evolving customer needs.

Balancing the Strength of Value Propositions Over Time

The FVP for the da Vinci Surgical System underscores a vital principle: The prominence of value propositions evolves with the customer archetype and stage of adoption. In its early life cycle, the system's CVP, revolutionizing surgical precision and improving patient outcomes, dominated the narrative. Early adopters, such as pioneering surgeons and innovative hospitals, were driven by the promise of clinical breakthroughs and the opportunity to advance medical practice.

As adoption expanded, financial considerations took center stage. Hospital administrators, tasked with budget oversight and ROI accountability, required tangible proof of the system's cost-effectiveness and scalability. Intuitive Surgical addressed these needs by presenting detailed economic analyses, highlighting cost savings from reduced hospital stays, increased procedural throughput, and enhanced reimbursement opportunities.

This shifting emphasis illustrates that no single value proposition can meet all customer needs at all times. Innovators must adapt their messaging to reflect the changing priorities of stakeholders. By initially emphasizing core benefits and later focusing on financial advantages, Intuitive Surgical successfully navigated the adoption curve, building trust and allegiance across its audience.

Financial clarity strengthens your business by establishing economic credibility and fostering strategic investment. However, true organizational success requires more than financial precision. It also depends on operational excellence. Tailoring Operational Value Propositions to the unique priorities of operational leaders helps innovation evolve into a driving force for efficiency, speed, and quality.

Enhancing Operational Value: Optimizing Efficiency

Operational Value Propositions (OVPs) focus on improving the efficiency, reliability, and overall performance of an organization's processes. Unlike FVPs, which emphasize cost and profitability, OVPs address how innovations optimize workflows, eliminate inefficiencies, and enhance the organization's ability to meet its objectives. By concentrating on elements such as time management, resource utilization, and quality control, OVPs become critical drivers of operational success and a cornerstone of customer satisfaction.

Operational Value in Action: Learning from Market Leaders

Successful organizations across industries have leveraged OVPs to drive unique value and distinguish themselves in the market. FedEx, Amazon, Chick-fil-A, and Starbucks showcase the transformative power of operational excellence, delivering seamless customer experiences and optimizing internal processes. FedEx delivers operational value through faster, more reliable service. Its focus on excellence consistently exceeds expectations for speed and precision.

FedEx exemplifies operational value by optimizing routes, reducing delivery times, and ensuring reliability. Its commitment to operational excellence consistently meets and exceeds customer expectations for speed and precision.[45]

Similarly, Amazon's Prime Now service highlighted operational value by integrating advanced technology and logistics to deliver products within hours. This emphasis on speed and reliability not only enhanced the customer experience but also solidified Amazon's market dominance. Amazon has used its extensive infrastructure and technology to redefine customer expectations for delivery times, making operational efficiency a key pillar of its success.

Another company that emphasizes operational value is Chick-fil-A, renowned for its quick service and exceptional quality. The company has streamlined its operations to minimize wait times without sacrificing standards. During the pandemic, Chick-fil-A showcased its adaptability through rapid adjustments to increased drive-through demand, maintaining operational efficiency and delivering strong customer satisfaction. This flexibility is a key component of their operational value, as they continuously adapt to changing circumstances to meet customer needs.

In the same vein, Starbucks revolutionized customer service through its mobile app, allowing patrons to order ahead and avoid long wait times. This integration of technology not only enhances the customer experience but also streamlines in-store operations, delivering consistent quality and convenience across all locations. Starbucks's ability to incorporate operational efficiencies into its service model is a key factor in its widespread success.[46]

In healthcare, the da Vinci Surgical System is an example of how operational value can directly impact patient care. The da Vinci system reduces hospital stays and recovery times for patients undergoing robotic procedures, which in turn optimizes hospital operations and resource utilization. These efficiencies align with hospitals' priorities for improved outcomes, better resource management, and operational cost savings. The da Vinci system's ability to enhance both patient care and operational flow exemplifies how operational value can transform industries.[47]

Value Prop.	Definition	Chick-fil-A	Starbucks	Robotic Surgery: 1999-2004
Operational	Enhances workflows, efficiency, and performance; addressing time, quality, and process improvements	Efficient drive-throughs, speedy service, and consistent quality standards	Streamlined ordering via mobile app and consistent product delivery	Shorter hospital stays and improved resource utilization through minimally invasive procedures

Aligning Operational Value Propositions with Operational Customers

Operational alignment is the backbone of innovation adoption *within* organizations. For operational decision makers such as operations managers, quality assurance directors, or process engineers, success depends on three critical pillars of efficiency, speed, and quality. These leaders are tasked with not only maintaining these standards but also driving continuous improvement to adapt to evolving demands.

Take the example of an operations manager in a manufacturing facility, tasked with ensuring uninterrupted production. Every moment of downtime translates into diminished output. Now imagine two vendors pitching solutions. One focuses on product features; the other delivers a tailored narrative that shows how their solution reduces downtime, streamlines workflows, and integrates effortlessly with existing systems. Naturally, the manager opts for the vendor who understands operational hurdles and presents actionable, relevant answers. Operational alignment transforms OVPs into tools that speak directly to the priorities of frontline decision-makers.

How well does your offering integrate into existing workflows or processes? Consider whether it creates efficiencies or introduces new complexities for your customers.

Crafting Value Propositions for Operational Customers

Crafting a compelling OVP requires addressing these priorities:

Step 1: Identifying Key Process Improvements

The foundation of a strong OVP lies in identifying and addressing specific inefficiencies or bottlenecks within the customer's operations. Operational customers value solutions that directly improve their processes, saving time, reducing complexity, and optimizing resource use. To craft an OVP that resonates, begin by pinpointing specific inefficiencies or bottlenecks within the customer's operations. Engage operational teams directly to map workflows and uncover pain points that disrupt efficiency. For example, a warehouse management system provider might demonstrate how its software enhances inventory tracking and reduces picking errors, enabling faster and more accurate order fulfillment.

Step 2: Measuring the Impact on Performance

Operational customers demand clear, measurable evidence of how your innovation improves performance metrics. The ability to demonstrate quantifiable outcomes, such as reduced downtime or increased throughput, is critical to building a compelling case for adoption. Highlight measurable outcomes that validate your solution's performance. For instance, MedTrans Go might showcase how its services help hospitals reduce medical cancellations due to transportation or interpretation issues, directly improving patient care and hospital efficiency.

Step 3: Focusing on Integration and Compatibility

Operational customers are particularly sensitive to the potential disruptions that new solutions might cause to their existing workflows. A strong OVP highlights smooth integration and straightforward implementation to build confidence in the adoption process. Emphasize how your solution works well with existing systems and workflows. For example, a project management software provider might showcase its compatibility with platforms like Slack or Microsoft Teams making the learning curve manageable and avoiding disruptions to ongoing operations.

Operational leaders prioritize efficiency and reliability. How does your offering minimize disruptions during implementation and deliver consistent performance over time?

Achieving Alignment: Why It Matters

Operational customers don't just appreciate a good fit. They expect it. When your OVP clicks with their reality, it's not a bonus, it's the baseline. When alignment is achieved, it enables:

- » Targeted Efficiency: Solutions address specific operational bottlenecks, optimizing workflows and removing barriers to productivity.
- » Enhanced Resource Utilization: Customers maximize output with minimal input, leading to better allocation of time, materials, and staffing.
- » Quality Assurance: Robust OVPs integrate quality control mechanisms that deliver consistent, high-standard outputs aligned with or exceeding expectations.
- » Increased Productivity: Teams achieve more with less effort, improving morale, fostering innovation, and maintaining strong day-to-day performance.
- » Scalable Operations: Solutions scale effectively with growth.
- » Accelerated Market Delivery: Faster, more reliable workflows shorten production cycles.

With these principles in mind, it's clear that OVPs occupy a unique position within CFOSS. They address critical aspects of efficiency and process optimization, but presenting them in isolation can risk unintended consequences. The Five-Finger Model provides a cautionary lens for understanding how operational value interacts with and complements other dimensions of value creation, supporting a balanced and effective approach to delivering customer impact.

The Five-Finger Model Revisited: Operational Value in Balance

The middle finger in the Five Finger CFOSS Model represents the OVP and serves as the stabilizing force within the framework. However, as noted earlier, focusing solely on operational value much like displaying a raised middle finger can risk alienating customers. The OVP is essential for addressing inefficiencies and optimizing processes. However, it must be carefully framed, and often combined with other value propositions, to prevent unintended consequences.

An OVP can highlight inefficiencies, reduce errors, or improve input-output ratios, but when presented in isolation, it can imply the customer is not managing operations well. Framing these improvements within a broader value narrative is essential to avoid alienating operational stakeholders. Operational customers value improvements but also take pride in the systems and efforts they've already built. A conversation focused exclusively on operational shortcomings can feel like a critique, triggering defensiveness rather than receptiveness.

This risk underscores an important caveat. The OVP is most effective when softened or complemented by other value propositions. For example, combining the OVP (middle finger) with the FVP (index finger) creates a peace sign approach that communicates, "We can help you save money by saving time." This combined narrative is less about pointing out flaws and more about highlighting opportunities for mutual success.

The peace sign analogy emphasizes collaboration rather than critique. When discussing operational improvements, linking the conversation to financial gains or core mission alignment helps customers perceive the value as enhancing their goals rather than simply addressing issues. It shifts the focus from what's not working to what could work better, fostering a sense of partnership rather than judgment.

Consider Bugle, a company focused on simplifying the volunteer experience for nonprofits. Rather than criticizing a nonprofit's current volunteer management system, Bugle highlights the added value of their software by saying, "Our platform streamlines event coordination, helps you engage more volunteers, and boosts your impact by making the process easier for everyone involved."[48] This approach blends operational improvements, such as simplifying event management, with the core value of increasing community engagement and organizational mission alignment, ultimately empowering nonprofits to enhance their reach and effectiveness.

Or take a sales representative presenting robotic surgery technology to a surgeon. Rather than focusing too heavily on how the surgeon's current methods lead to excessive blood loss, which might feel like a critique of their expertise, the rep reframes the conversation saying, "The robotic system is designed to enhance precision and reduce blood loss, which translates to faster recovery times for your patients and shorter hospital stays. This not only improves outcomes but also optimizes your operating room schedule and resource use." By combining operational benefits with broader value, the rep avoids creating defensiveness and fosters collaboration.

Operational alignment delivers gains in efficiency; however, achieving long-term growth and market leadership requires something more.

Harnessing Strategic Value: Gaining Competitive Advantage

Strategic Value Propositions (SVPs) serve as the forward-looking pillar of the CFOSS framework. SVPs focus on broader organizational ambitions, achieving market leadership, entering new markets, or future-proofing operations.

Where OVPs center on process efficiencies, SVPs emphasize how organizations leverage their unique strengths and assets to carve out a distinctive market position. SVPs highlight how an offering can help customers seize opportunities. This requires comprehension of both customer ambitions and the broader competitive environment.

Strategic Value in Action: Learning from Market Leaders

Market leaders across industries provide compelling examples of how SVPs drive differentiation and growth by aligning their offerings with customer ambitions and market trends.

Firehouse Subs and Coca-Cola: Innovating Customer Experience

The partnership between Firehouse Subs and Coca-Cola to introduce the Freestyle beverage dispenser in 2007 was more than a technological upgrade.[49] It was a strategic play to enhance customer satisfaction and distinguish the brand in a crowded fast-casual market. Firehouse Subs offered an unprecedented level of drink customization, reinforcing its commitment to innovation and a distinctive dining experience.

This approach supported the company's strategic goals in two key ways. It strengthened brand differentiation and built deeper customer loyalty. The introduction of the Freestyle machine positioned Firehouse Subs as a forward-thinking brand willing to embrace cutting-edge technology. But what truly elevated the experience was the exclusive Firehouse Cherry Lime-Aid, a signature drink you could only get at Firehouse Subs, made possible through the Freestyle system. This unique offering transformed a standard beverage choice into a brand-specific experience, setting Firehouse apart from competitors and creating a sense of ownership over the customer interaction.

In a market where customization is no longer optional but expected, Firehouse Subs met and exceeded evolving consumer demands. The wide array of drink choices, including exclusive, branded flavors, allowed customers to tailor their experience to their preferences, fostering a sense of agency and personal connection to the brand. This emotional engagement translated into higher satisfaction and repeat visits, aligning directly with Firehouse's long-term strategic objective of cultivating a loyal customer base.

The Freestyle partnership was not a one-off initiative. In 2019, Firehouse doubled down by introducing the next-generation Freestyle 9100 during its twenty-fifth anniversary celebration, further signaling an enduring commitment to innovation and customer-centricity.[50]

Through this integration of technology and branding, Firehouse Subs did more than improve operational efficiency. It strategically aligned its offerings to elevate customer engagement, strengthen differentiation, and drive sustainable market leadership.

Chick-fil-A: A Principled Approach to Strategic Positioning

Chick-fil-A exemplifies the strength of aligning strategy with deeply held values. Its decision to remain closed on Sundays, a policy grounded in the religious beliefs of its founder, S. Truett Cathy, has become a defining element of its SVP.[51] This decision might appear counterintuitive due to potential revenue loss, yet it has cultivated a loyal customer base that respects the brand's commitment to its principles.

This alignment with core values has proven to be a strategic advantage. Chick-fil-A's non-mall-franchised locations generate average annual sales of $8.7 million, outpacing even high-performing competitors like McDonald's.[52] By staying true to its principles and delivering consistent performance, Chick-fil-A has solidified its long-term competitive positioning in the fast-food industry.

Starbucks: Scaling with Strategy and Technology

Starbucks has built its strategic value by leveraging technology to deepen customer engagement and scale globally. The Starbucks Rewards program exemplifies its commitment to fostering customer faithfulness through personalized incentives. Beyond driving repeat business, this program equips Starbucks with valuable customer data, enabling the company to refine marketing strategies and tailor the customer experience.

On a global scale, Starbucks's licensing model has enabled expansion into new markets and delivered high returns on invested capital. By partnering with local operators and adapting to regional dynamics, Starbucks has grown its presence to more than seventeen thousand licensed stores worldwide.[53]

Robotic Surgery: A Strategic Leap in Healthcare

Between 1999 and 2004, the adoption of robotic surgery highlighted the strategic value of innovation in healthcare. Hospitals that integrated robotic systems like the da Vinci Surgical System gained a significant competitive edge by positioning themselves as leaders in minimally invasive surgery.[54]

Early adopters such as the Vattikuti Urology Institute, under the leadership of Dr. Mani Menon, leveraged robotic surgery to attract top-tier surgical talent and increase patient demand. Dr. Vip Patel shared that the demand for robotic procedures surged beyond expectations, with patients actively seeking out hospitals that offered this advanced technology, solidifying these institutions' reputations as centers of excellence.[55]

This strategic positioning had a ripple effect, enhancing hospital branding and increasing procedural revenues. The da Vinci Surgical System became synonymous with cutting-edge care, providing hospitals with a unique competitive advantage. By aligning their offerings with advancements in technology, these hospitals demonstrated how SVPs can redefine market leadership and drive long-term growth.

Value Prop.	Definition	Chick-fil-A	Starbucks	Robotic Surgery: 1999-2004
Strategic	The value generated by achieving a competitive advantage through differentiation or market positioning	A unique brand identity and values-driven approach distinguishes it within the competitive fast-food landscape	Adaptation to changing consumer trends, expansion into new markets	The capacity for hospitals to innovate and create unique value, coupled with the influence on surgeon satisfaction and patient demand

Aligning Strategic Value Propositions with Strategic Customers

In the fast-paced business world, aligning SVPs with Visionary Trailblazers goes beyond being advantageous. Decision-makers, such as CEOs,

CTOs, and strategic planning directors, operate with a forward-looking perspective. They are focused on sustained growth, market leadership, and resilience against evolving challenges.

SVPs differentiate themselves by addressing these future-oriented goals, positioning innovations as enablers of transformation and long-term value creation. Strategic alignment means demonstrating how your offering integrates into the customer's broader narrative of supporting innovation and driving growth beyond immediate needs.

Consider a CEO preparing for a pivotal board meeting. Their task is to present a comprehensive strategy for market expansion and enhanced brand equity. Among their choices are two potential partners. One offers a tactical solution focused on short-term improvements. The other delivers a proposal outlining how their partnership will empower the company to break into new markets, lead in innovation, and establish a competitive edge that endures. The CEO, guided by the company's broader ambitions, chooses the latter.

Strategic alignment transforms value propositions into tools for vision realization. It shifts the focus from transactional benefits to a collaborative journey of growth and adaptation. For innovators and entrepreneurs, aligning SVPs with strategic customers enables them to exceed expectations and offer a road map for shared success that spans years, not months.

How does your Strategic Value Proposition prepare customers for long-term growth and market leadership? Could this be communicated more clearly or compellingly?

Crafting Value Propositions for Strategic Customers

Strategic customers operate with a forward-looking perspective, prioritizing competitive differentiation, market leadership, and long-term growth. Crafting an SVP that resonates with these visionary customers requires a grasp of their goals and a clear demonstration of how your offering aligns with their strategic vision.

To create compelling SVPs for strategic customers, follow this structured three-step process:

Step 1: Define the Strategic Advantage

Strategic customers are focused on how your innovation elevates their position within the marketplace or industry. Your SVP must articulate the unique advantage(s) your offering delivers. Identify and communicate the specific ways your innovation positions the customer for market leadership or industry impact. For example, an EdTech solution could help a university lead the charge in AI-integrated learning, positioning them as a model for 21st-century curriculum innovation.

Step 2: Highlight Long-Term Growth Potential

Strategic customers need to see how your solution supports their vision for long-term growth. Show how your solution delivers scalable, sustainable benefits. For instance, a fitness tech company launching a wearable device with virtual coaching might highlight its role in building a loyal customer base, boosting subscription revenue, and positioning the brand at the forefront of health tech trends. This framing connects the device to the company's long-term objectives, presenting it as a key driver of competitive advantage.

Step 3: Align with Strategic Mission and Vision

For strategic customers, the most resonant value propositions align with their overarching mission and vision. Your SVP must tie your innovation to their broader purpose, creating a narrative that reinforces their commitment to transformative goals. Think of this alignment like the ring finger in the value proposition hand. It's what holds everything together and gives the value proposition deeper meaning.

Demonstrate how your offering integrates with the customer's mission and contributes to achieving their vision. Consider a renewable energy company proposing large-scale solar installations to a city government. Framing the project as a direct contributor to the city's sustainability goals and its pursuit of national leadership in green energy, the company positions its offering as a vital component of the customer's broader environmental mission.

Achieving Alignment: Why It Matters

Alignment between SVPs and strategic customers is critical for long-term organizational success. Resonant SVPs empower strategic customers to achieve growth, sustain competitive advantage, and shape their industries. This alignment unlocks:

- » **Market Differentiation**: Aligned SVPs position strategic customers as market leaders through innovation, disruption, and exceptional customer experiences.
- » **Customer Loyalty and Retention**: Strong SVPs build trust and transform relationships into partnerships.
- » **Enhanced Brand Value**: SVPs that emphasize leadership and innovation elevate both your brand and the brand value of strategic customers.
- » **Higher Market Share**: Strategic customer endorsements drive adoption and expand reach.
- » **Pricing Premium**: Aligned SVPs may justify premium pricing by demonstrating value.
- » **Sustainable Competitive Advantage:** SVPs create unique advantages, such as proprietary technology or exclusive partnerships, that are difficult for competitors to replicate.
- » **Attracting Strategic Partnerships:** Compelling SVPs foster collaboration, leading to co-innovation, new market access, and shared growth.
- » **Long-Term Growth and Scalability:** Strategic alignment supports mutual expansion, securing extended contracts and deeper collaborations.
- » **Influence on Industry Trends:** Aligned SVPs position your solutions as benchmarks for innovation, driving industry standards and reinforcing relevance.

Strategic alignment addresses the forward-looking goals of visionary customers. But, the ability to align with community values is becoming increasingly critical in today's socially conscious world. Social Value Propositions connect business outcomes with the expectations of socially aware customers.

Fostering Social Value: Building Community

The Social Value Proposition (SoVP) represents a significant and evolving shift in how businesses conceptualize and create value. Unlike CVPs, which focus on delivering direct benefits to individual customers, or FVPs, which emphasize economic advantages, SoVPs prioritize generating positive societal impacts. These can encompass addressing community needs, improving social equity, enhancing sustainability, or fostering long-term societal development, etc.

SoVPs integrate societal value into the heart of organizational strategy. This approach aligns with stakeholder capitalism, as championed by Edward Freeman, who highlights the interdependence between business success and societal well-being. Freeman, in a presentation at Georgia State University, stressed the importance of creating win-win outcomes, urging businesses to balance profitability with broader community interests.[56] SoVPs operationalize this philosophy by embedding social value into the decision-making process, fostering inclusive and ethical practices that resonate with stakeholders.

Addressing societal needs enables SoVPs to establish genuine connections with socially conscious customers, employees, and partners. Connecting organizational strategies with values such as environmental responsibility and ethical governance has become increasingly critical as customers and stakeholders prioritize these principles in their purchasing, employment, and collaboration decisions.[57]

Social Value in Action: Learning from Market Leaders

Many businesses demonstrate the transformative potential of SoVPs. Patagonia exemplifies a deep commitment to environmental stewardship through its mission to "save our home planet," setting a benchmark for socially conscious businesses.[58] Sustainability is woven into every facet of its operations, from utilizing recycled materials in its products to supporting grassroots environmental activism via its Patagonia Action Works platform. By aligning its operations with environmental advocacy, Patagonia not only reduces its ecological footprint but also cultivates loyalty among environmentally conscious consumers.

Ben & Jerry's has long championed social justice causes, embedding activism into its business ethos. The company leverages its platform to amplify critical social issues such as climate change and racial equity. Initiatives like creating flavors tied to social justice campaigns, such as Justice ReMix'd, link product offerings to broader societal goals, connecting deeply with socially conscious consumers.[59] Beyond advocacy, Ben & Jerry's actively invests in underserved communities, supporting local farmers and suppliers to create equitable economic opportunities. This integration of social equity into its supply chain aligns the company's operations with its core values.

TOMS Shoes revolutionized the business model for social outcomes with its One for One initiative, donating a pair of shoes to someone in need for every pair sold. This approach not only addresses immediate needs but also contributes to long-term community development by improving access to education and healthcare. By purchasing TOMS products, customers become active participants in creating positive change, fostering a shared sense of purpose and enhancing brand loyalty.[60]

The Russell Innovation Center for Entrepreneurs illustrates how SoVPs can drive systemic change. As we discussed in chapter 3, RICE has created an ecosystem that fosters economic equity and community advancement. The center's initiatives have supported thousands of entrepreneurs and generated millions in economic impact.

These examples highlight how organizations effectively embed SoVPs into their strategies, leveraging their values to drive both societal and economic benefits.

Value Prop.	Definition	Patagonia	Ben & Jerry's	TOMS Shoes	RICE
Social	The societal impact created through the innovation or service, emphasizing equity, sustainability, and community development	Reducing environmental impact through sustainable practices	Advocating for racial equity and climate action through activism and supply chain inclusivity	Addressing basic needs and fostering global development through a giving-based model	Advancing economic equity by empowering underserved entrepreneurs

How does your offering contribute to broader societal goals? Reflect on whether these contributions are effectively communicated to your stakeholders.

Aligning Social Value Propositions with Social Customers

Customers increasingly gravitate toward brands that support meaningful causes and demonstrate genuine commitments to making a positive impact. Social alignment involves authentic actions and clear narratives that demonstrate a company's dedication to addressing societal issues.

Consider a consumer choosing between two products. Both are comparable in price and quality; however, one emphasizes sustainability and ethical sourcing, whereas the other does not. The socially conscious consumer will likely choose the brand that aligns with their values, reinforcing their belief that their purchase contributes to a greater cause. This shift highlights the importance of matching SoVPs with social customers' priorities.

Crafting Value Propositions for Social Customers

Developing impactful SoVPs involves recognizing how your customers' goals intersect with broader societal movements and then fitting your offering with those shared values. Remember, Network Ambassadors prioritize impact over personal or organizational benefits. They value innovations that address systemic challenges, foster community well-being, or advance environmental sustainability.

To craft compelling SoVPs for social customers, follow these three steps:

Step 1: Identify the Broader Societal Impact

Social customers evaluate innovations based on their potential to address critical societal challenges. Clearly defining your offering's social impact demonstrates its alignment with the priorities of these customers. For instance, a company introducing biodegradable packaging appeals to environmentally conscious retailers.

Step 2: Demonstrate Authentic Commitment to Purpose

Social customers are highly attuned to authenticity. Demonstrate that your organization prioritizes societal benefits as a core part of its mission, not merely as a marketing strategy. For example, a beverage company launching a clean water initiative establishes credibility by transparently sharing impact metrics, such as the number of communities served or gallons of clean water delivered.

Step 3: Align with Customer Values and Movements

Social customers often align their purchasing decisions with movements or causes they support. Connect to these values, showing how your innovation supports broader societal shifts such as climate action, social justice, or economic empowerment. For instance, an ethically focused fashion brand appeals to advocates of fair labor practices by highlighting its commitment to fair wages, safe working conditions, and reduced environmental impact. Social customers see their purchases as reflections of their principles.

Achieving Alignment: Why It Matters

Alignment between SoVPs and social customers is transformative in today's purpose-driven market. This kind of alignment produces:

- **Brand Loyalty and Trust:** Authentic SoVPs rooted in shared values build relationships that extend beyond transactions, creating loyal advocates who support both the mission and the brand.
- **Stronger Community Connections:** Businesses that prioritize SoVPs connect with communities, enhancing reputation and fostering goodwill.
- **Attraction and Retention of Purpose-Driven Talent:** Many employees are drawn to organizations that align with their values, creating an engaged and committed workforce driven by shared purpose.
- **Appeal to Socially Responsible Investors:** SoVPs may attract investors focused on balancing profit with societal impact.
- **Resilience Through Social Capital:** Strong ties with communities and stakeholders build trust and goodwill, providing stability and support during times of uncertainty.
- **Market Differentiation:** In competitive markets, values-driven businesses stand out.
- **Access to New Markets:** SoVPs enable businesses to connect with values-driven demographics, expanding their reach and engaging previously untapped audiences.

When companies align their SoVPs with the values of social customers, they unlock a powerful synergy that attracts talent, enhances community ties, and supports long-term sustainability. In doing so, they transform their business into a force for good, creating not only economic success but also societal impact.

Imagine your social customers sharing your solution's impact with others. What stories or outcomes would they highlight, and how might you amplify these through your Social Value Proposition?

The Pinky Finger: A Small but Powerful Force in Value Creation

SoVPs may not always be directly tied to immediate financial metrics, but they are foundational for fostering long-term value, strengthening community ties, and driving social progress. Through SoVPs, businesses establish stronger connections with their communities, enhance their reputations, and build enduring loyalty among socially conscious stakeholders. The pinky finger reminds us that true strength lies in purpose and contribution rather than size.

Orchestrating Holistic Value

The image below presents a framework that connects value propositions with corresponding customer characteristics across five key categories. Each value proposition aligns with a specific customer archetype, emphasizing the distinct priorities of each group.

	CORE CUSTOMER	FINANCIAL CUSTOMER	OPERATIONAL CUSTOMER	STRATEGIC CUSTOMER	SOCIAL CUSTOMER
CORE VP (CVP)	Aligns well with their focus on solving fundamental problems effectively				
FINANCIAL VP (FVP)		Highly relevant; driven by ROI and financial benefits			
OPERATIONAL VP (OVP)			Aligns well with their focus on optimizing processes and efficiency		
STRATEGIC VP (SVP)				Aligns well with their focus on innovation and competitive advantage	
SOCIAL VP (SoVP)					Aligns well with their focus on generating positive social impact and shared values

Each CFOSS construct delivers distinct benefits, but their true power emerges through integration. Much like an orchestra, where individual instruments combine to create a harmonious performance, the CFOSS framework achieves its greatest impact when Core, Financial, Operational, Strategic, and Social Value Propositions work in concert. Entrepreneurs who master this integration can deliver offerings that meet diverse customer needs and unlock exceptional success.

What happens when you focus solely on one dimension of value (e.g., financial or operational) without considering the others?

Consider the analogy of splinting a pinky finger. Supporting a single finger requires accounting for its interdependence with the others.

Similarly, a value proposition that focuses solely on financial outcomes without considering operational efficiency or core customer benefits risks being incomplete. CFOSS offers the flexibility to adapt and combine constructs.

Illustrative Combinations

1. **Core, Operational, and Social: Holistic Impact.** For example, Acivilate's platform Pokket focuses on reducing recidivism by supporting populations transitioning from incarceration to stable community life. It integrates medical and behavioral care summaries (core), enhances data access to facilitate better decision-making and coordination among service providers (operational), and fosters stability for vulnerable communities by addressing critical social determinants of health and well-being (social).[61] This comprehensive and compassionate solution bridges gaps in care and support, empowering individuals to rebuild their lives while reducing societal costs associated with reentry challenges.

2. **Financial and Operational:** Harmonizing Effect. A cloud-based workforce management platform highlights this pairing by reducing overhead costs (financial) while integrating seamlessly with existing HR and payroll systems (operational), enabling organizations to scale efficiently without disrupting workflows.

3. **The Shaka Impact.** Inspired by the Hawaiian gesture symbolizing friendship and unity, the shaka impact illustrates the fusion of core and social value. Global health efforts to combat open defecation address disease prevention as a core value and foster dignity and equity for disadvantaged communities as a social value).[62] This integration advances public health.

4. **All Five Constructs.** The Quintessential Punch. Robotic surgery during its early adoption years serves as a stellar example. By aligning:
   » Core value (minimally invasive procedures),
   » Financial value (cost savings through reduced hospital stays),
   » Operational value (increased patient throughput),
   » Strategic value (market leadership in surgical innovation), and
   » Social value (inclusive approaches benefiting diverse patient populations), robotic surgery systems became the epitome of CFOSS in action, offering comprehensive value.

> *In your current offerings, where do you see the potential for a CFOSS fist approach—integrating all five constructs into a unified, impactful narrative? What would it take to align these dimensions in your value proposition?*

Achieving CFOSS alignment is not a one-time effort—it is a dynamic process of refinement and adaptation. Although mastering alignment is essential, anticipating and navigating potential missteps is equally critical. Misalignment can disrupt customer relationships, hinder innovation adoption, and stall growth. Understanding and addressing these dynamics helps keep your strategy robust and adaptable. In chapter 5, we'll explore the pitfalls of misalignment in depth.

CHAPTER 4 IN REVIEW

- » Core Value Propositions (CVPs): Represent the mission and purpose of an organization, anchoring it in differentiation and fostering customer loyalty.
- » Core alignment builds trust and establishes a foundation for integration by addressing the most pressing challenges and connecting with professional missions.
- » Financial Value Propositions (FVPs): Provide measurable economic benefits like cost savings and ROI, offering clear value for financially focused customers.
- » Financial alignment demonstrates measurable economic impact, manages risks, and validates scalability to position innovation as an indispensable investment.
- » Operational Value Propositions (OVPs): Focus on efficiency and seamless integration, balancing practicality with collaborative improvement.
- » Operational alignment reduces inefficiencies, integrates systems smoothly, and drives productivity.
- » Strategic Value Propositions (SVPs): Highlight competitive advantages and long-term growth, aligning with visionary customer goals and market leadership.
- » Strategic alignment fosters market leadership, competitive differentiation, and long-term partnerships by aligning with broader strategic goals.
- » Social Value Propositions (SoVPs): Emphasize societal impact, addressing community needs and fostering loyalty among socially conscious stakeholders.
- » Social alignment builds trust and allegiance by authentically reflecting societal values, creating meaningful connections, and fostering community relationships.
- » Combined value propositions: Successful businesses leverage CFOSS combinations to create comprehensive solutions.
- » Effective CFOSS alignment requires tailored value propositions for each archetype and a cohesive integration of all dimensions to drive synergy.

Scan to watch the Chapter Overview Video.
Get a quick summary, key insights, and what to look for in the upcoming chapter.

CHAPTER 05

Let there be consistency in whatever you do and whatever you say. If what you think and say is mismatching with what you do, you can't really be trusted.
—Israelmore Ayivor, Shaping the Dream

The Hazards of Mismatching

Fit is far from guaranteed. Conflicting priorities, unclear messaging, or a poor grasp of customer needs can seriously undermine business success. In this chapter, we analyze the dangers of CFOSS® mismatches by exploring how and why they occur and offering actionable insights for identifying, addressing, and preventing these pitfalls.

CFOSS mismatches arise when value propositions fail to meet the needs, expectations, or priorities of their intended customer archetypes. Each CFOSS dimension provides an opportunity to connect meaningfully with customers, but misalignment turns these opportunities into challenges.

Consider the risks of a mismatch. Presenting a FVP to a customer primarily driven by social priorities creates friction and confusion. Similarly, emphasizing OVP to strategic decision-makers focused on market positioning may lead to disengagement. These missteps disrupt the harmony needed for adoption and advocacy. At this stage, recognizing how mismatches emerge and the risks they carry is critical.

Dangers of CFOSS Mismatches

Even small disconnects in CFOSS alignment can escalate fast. They divert time, waste effort, and undermine customer relationships, often causing hesitation, reduced buy-in, and slower. Below are some of the most common pitfalls that arise when CFOSS elements are out of sync.

1. **Prolonged Sales Cycles:** Misaligned value propositions add friction to the sales process.
2. **Increased Cost of Sales:** When propositions fail to resonate, acquiring customers requires greater effort.
3. **Reduced Conversion Rates:** Even strong initial interest can falter if mismatched propositions alienate prospects.
4. **High Customer Turnover:** Misalignment affects customer acquisition and retention. Customers who feel underserved or misled are more likely to leave.
5. **Stifled Revenue Growth:** Misalignment suffocates upselling and cross-selling opportunities.
6. **Lower Early-Stage Valuations:** Startups face heightened risks from misalignment. Investors prioritize clear product-market fit. Misaligned propositions may raise doubts or increase risk, lowering valuations and reducing funding opportunities.
7. **Poor Customer Adoption:** Even innovative solutions can fail if misalignment creates barriers.

What are the potential consequences of misaligned value propositions for your innovation?

The early-stage adoption struggles outlined in chapter 1, long sales cycles, high churn rates, and missed revenue opportunities, often stem from disconnects between value propositions and what customers truly need. These breakdowns slow momentum and reintroduce the very obstacles businesses work hard to avoid. Achieving resonance between your offering and customer priorities is not a one-time effort but a continuous process.

Examples of CFOSS Mismatches

Sustainability vs. Performance: Patagonia's Social Value Mismatch

Patagonia's dedication to environmental sustainability and social impact has built a strong reputation among ethically conscious consumers. Its eco-friendly practices and activism appeal to customers who prioritize sustainability.

However, Patagonia's emphasis on its SoVP can conflict with the expectations of core customers like outdoor professionals and adventurers who prioritize performance and durability. For these customers, high-performance gear for extreme conditions often takes precedence, and sustainability initiatives that overshadow performance innovation may leave them underserved.

Patagonia excels at engaging socially conscious audiences, yet sustaining leadership across diverse markets requires balancing sustainability goals with technical innovation to meet the expectations of all archetypes.

Value vs. Values: Apple's Financial Misalignment

Apple's premium offerings are known for innovation, sleek design, and superior user experiences, which strongly appeal to loyal customers who prioritize technology and brand prestige. However, its pricing strategy often conflicts with the priorities of financial customers who emphasize cost-effectiveness and return on investment.

Budget-conscious individuals and small businesses may struggle to justify the initial high costs of Apple products, even when the ecosystem benefits and product longevity offer long-term value. Competing brands like Dell and HP offer similar functionality at a lower price point, drawing financial customers away.

To bridge this gap, Apple explores financing solutions and secondary market offerings to appeal to cost-sensitive customers without diluting its brand identity.

Beyond Budget Travel: Southwest Airlines' Strategic Misalignment

Southwest Airlines has built a strong FVP around affordability and operational efficiency, making it a top choice for individual travelers and small businesses. However, this focus on low-cost travel limits its appeal to corporate clients with strategic needs.[63]

Corporate customers often seek premium services like business-class seating, global travel alliances, and comprehensive travel solutions. Southwest's no-frills approach and lack of international partnerships make it less attractive to companies looking for travel solutions that align with their brand image.

Recognizing this gap, Southwest recently announced plans to introduce tailored premium services, including assigned seating and premium options with added comfort, expected to roll out by 2026.[64] These changes aim to better cater to business travelers and preserve its strong FVP. Additionally, the airline is exploring international partnerships to enhance its global connectivity, with its first collaboration launching in 2025. Southwest demonstrates how evolving its model to meet strategic customer needs can expand its appeal.

Ethics Over Efficiency: Uber's Social Misalignment

Uber's operational efficiency and convenience attract users seeking hassle-free travel. However, its focus on cost-effectiveness often clashes with the priorities of socially conscious customers who value ethical practices and corporate responsibility.

Concerns over driver pay, lack of benefits, and environmental impact create significant misalignment with social customers. Advocacy for fair labor practices and regulatory compliance has put Uber under scrutiny, raising doubts about its commitment to community well-being.[65] Balancing operational efficiency with ethical practices helps Uber rebuild trust among socially conscious users and strengthen its SoVP.

These examples highlight the risks of CFOSS misalignment and the consequences of failing to meet diverse customer needs. Businesses must view misalignment as an opportunity for improvement, adapting strategies to address gaps and create holistic value for all customer archetypes.

Sustainable success depends on intentional alignment, which enables the CFOSS dimensions to function cohesively in addressing the needs of diverse audiences. For a deeper understanding of how misalignments manifested in the early adoption of robotic surgery, refer to Appendix D, which provides a detailed analysis of the effects of these mismatches in the context of the da Vinci Surgical System.

How can customer feedback help you identify and address mismatches in your approach?

The likelihood of misalignment far outweighs that of perfect alignment, underscoring the need for deliberate effort and focus. Successful alignment isn't automatic. It requires a nuanced understanding of customer archetypes and tailored value propositions.

Avoiding CFOSS Mismatches: A Proactive Approach

The table below highlights the inherent complexity of CFOSS alignment, showcasing the twenty-five potential interactions between value propositions and customer archetypes. Among these, only five represent ideal matches where the value proposition aligns seamlessly with the customer's specific priorities. The remaining twenty scenarios reflect potential mismatches, each presenting distinct risks and challenges. These misalignments can create friction throughout the customer journey.

	CORE CUSTOMER	FINANCIAL CUSTOMER	OPERATIONAL CUSTOMER	STRATEGIC CUSTOMER	SOCIAL CUSTOMER
CORE VALUE PROPOSITION (CVP)	Aligns well with their focus on solving fundamental problems effectively	Less impactful as they prioritize financial metrics over core problem-solving	Interested but needs clarity on how it integrates with existing processes	Seeks alignment with long-term strategic goals and differentiation	Appreciates alignment with community benefits but not a primary driver
FINANCIAL VALUE PROPOSITION (FVP)	Less relevant; they focus more on solving core issues than on cost savings	Highly relevant; driven by ROI and financial benefits	Needs clear data on how financial savings translate to operational efficiency	Prioritizes competitive advantage over immediate financial gains	Skeptical; requires a strong business case for social responsibility
OPERATIONAL VALUE PROPOSITION (OVP)	Prioritizes solutions that address fundamental problems, rather than focusing on integration or workflow concerns	Needs to see how operational improvements lead to cost savings	Aligns well with their focus on optimizing processes and efficiency	Interested in market differentiation, rather than existing process efficiency	Concerned about potential negative impacts on the community despite efficiency gains
STRATEGIC VALUE PROPOSITION (SVP)	Wants solutions to immediate problems over long-term advantages and market leadership	Interested in demonstrable ROI and cost savings, versus emphasis on market leadership and long-term growth and competitive advantage	Needs to see how the solution avoids disruptions	Aligns well with their focus on innovation and competitive advantage	Interested in alignment with community values and contribution to the greater good
SOCIAL VALUE PROPOSITION (SOVP)	Focuses on the solution's impact on their work rather than social aspects	Requires a strong business case for social initiatives; may need financial justification	Values social impact if it aligns with operational goals and doesn't compromise efficiency	Interested in social impact that enhances brand reputation and long-term sustainability	Aligns well with their focus on generating positive social impact and shared values

The Innovation Adoption Pathway (IAP) introduced in chapter 1 offers a dynamic framework to address these challenges, emphasizing intentional connection with customer needs and the factors that influence adoption. Later chapters built on these principles by providing strategies for achieving CFOSS alignment:

» **Understanding Customer Archetypes:** Research the needs and motivations of all five customer types to tailor value propositions effectively.

» **Crafting Multi-dimensional Value Propositions:** Address the unique needs of each archetype by developing value propositions that deliver meaningful impact across all CFOSS dimensions.

» **Continuous Refinement:** Embrace alignment as an ongoing, adaptive process, using regular feedback and insights to refine and enhance your value propositions.

These principles lay the groundwork, but avoiding CFOSS mismatches demands actionable strategies. Below, we explore common alignment missteps and provide solutions to overcome them.

Common Missteps and Strategic Solutions

1. **Rushing to Acquire Customers Without Proper Vetting:** In the quest to rapidly grow market share, businesses often prioritize speed over strategic fit. For example, a SaaS startup promoting a project management tool broadly might attract enterprise clients who expect advanced features that the product, designed for freelancers, cannot deliver. This leads to prolonged sales cycles, increased customer acquisition costs, and higher churn thereby undermining growth

   Strategic Solution: Treat customer acquisition as a strategic process rather than a numbers game. Implement rigorous vetting mechanisms that go beyond demographics, focusing on specific needs and alignment with CFOSS dimensions.

2. **Expanding Too Quickly Without Addressing Nuances:** Rapid expansion into new markets or product lines without fully understanding new market customer nuances often backfires. Consider a sustainable fashion brand branching into furniture without adapting its logistics. Delays, inefficiencies, and unmet expectations lead to customer dissatisfaction.

   Strategic Solution: Adopt a measured growth strategy that builds on your core capabilities. Conduct thorough market research, evaluate operational readiness, and confirm that your infrastructure can support expansion. This deliberate approach mitigates risks, strengthens operational alignment, and promotes sustainable growth.

3. **Overlooking Customer Impact on the Business Model:** Each customer archetype engages with your business model differently, and ignoring these interactions can lead to mismatched offerings. For instance, a company targeting tech-savvy millennials with a voice assistant might struggle if it neglects their preference for mobile-first solutions over stationary devices.

   Strategic Solution: Evaluate how each customer archetype interacts with your business model. Analyze purchasing habits, usage patterns, and pain points to align offerings and projections. Apply these insights to plan effectively and sharpen CFOSS propositions for greater impact.

4. **Neglecting Customer Adoption Planning:** Even the most innovative products require thoughtful adoption strategies to succeed. A fitness app boasting advanced metrics may falter if users feel overwhelmed by its complexity or lack clear onboarding guidance.

   Strategic Solution: Develop adoption plans tailored to each CFOSS archetype, guiding customers through their unique user journeys.

Connecting the Dots

These missteps underscore the critical role of intentional alignment. They directly link to the TALC trap, funding-first trap, and indiscriminate pursuit discussed in chapter 1, where businesses risk spreading themselves too thin or prioritizing short-term gains over customer understanding. Avoiding these pitfalls requires businesses to approach CFOSS with deliberate focus.

What safeguards can you put in place to keep your offerings aligned with customer needs across all CFOSS dimensions?

Aligning CFOSS Propositions for Success

Alignment is dynamic, evolving in response to shifting markets, changing customer needs, and emerging challenges. Businesses that succeed are those that remain adaptable, responsive, and deeply connected to their customers. Continuous refinement, driven by data, feedback, and a commitment to understanding customer priorities, is the foundation of sustained success.

For further insights into the scenarios, behaviors, feelings, and concerns encountered during CFOSS alignments and misalignments, as well as how to align value propositions with specific customer archetypes, refer to Appendix C: CFOSS Archetype Value Matrix for a detailed breakdown.

Misalignment highlights the risks of dissonance across CFOSS value propositions. The path forward integrates the individual CFOSS dimensions into a unified framework, empowering you to orchestrate innovation adoption with precision and purpose.

As you step into the role of conductor, the lessons from previous chapters become your guiding score, helping you balance the unique needs of each customer archetype while maintaining a unified vision. This final chapter offers tools to help you compose a symphony of impact, where every note of your innovation resonates with clarity, coherence, and purpose.

CHAPTER 5 IN REVIEW

» Aligning CFOSS value propositions with customer archetypes is critical for fostering strong customer relationships and driving sustainable business growth.

» CFOSS mismatches lead to customer dissatisfaction, extended sales cycles, and stalled adoption.

» Misalignment occurs when value propositions fail to reflect the specific needs, priorities, or expectations of their intended customer archetypes.

» The consequences of misalignment include higher churn rates, reduced revenue potential, and missed opportunities for upselling or cross-selling.

» Preventing mismatches requires robust customer profiling, personalized strategies, and a commitment to iterating based on continuous feedback.

» Achieving successful CFOSS alignment demands flexibility and adaptability to evolving markets, shifting customer priorities, and emerging challenges.

138 | CUSTOMER ADOPTION REIMAGINED

Scan to watch the Chapter Overview Video.
Get a quick summary, key insights, and what to look for in the upcoming chapter.

CHAPTER 06

One band, one sound.
—Dr. Lee, Drumline

Mastering Your CFOSS® Symphony

As we've explored, CFOSS misalignment can create formidable barriers to adoption, but it also offers a unique opportunity to reimagine success. In this chapter, we move from diagnosing missteps to orchestrating a framework for impactful adoption strategies.

The preceding chapters have unpacked the five dimensions of CFOSS emphasizing their pivotal role in aligning value propositions. Now, as we reach the finale, it's time to integrate these elements into a cohesive strategy that equips you to harmonize your innovation with customer priorities.

Think of the CFOSS framework as a carefully composed symphony, with your innovation as the central composition. Your diverse customer archetypes represent the orchestra, each bringing unique contributions and perspectives. As the conductor, your task is to harmonize these elements into a coordinated melody that resonates with your audience, inspiring adoption.

> *How can you act as a conductor to harmonize the diverse priorities of your customer archetypes? Reflect on how you can balance different CFOSS dimensions to create a unified adoption strategy.*

The Innovation Adoption Pathway

This five-step guide empowers you to apply the CFOSS framework to your innovation, offering a road map to align value propositions with customer needs and achieve market success.

Step 1: Identify the Innovation

Define your innovation and the problem it solves or the opportunity it creates.

Step 2: Tuning Into Your Audience

Identify your CFOSS customer archetypes and their unique priorities related to your innovation.
- **Core Customers:** Value performance and problem solving
- **Financial Customers:** Prioritize economic returns
- **Operational Customers:** Seek seamless implementation
- **Strategic Customers:** Focus on competitive positioning
- **Social Customers:** Align with community impact

This insight sharpens your approach, allowing each message to connect with greater impact.

Step 3: Composing the Value Proposition

Craft targeted value propositions for each CFOSS dimension:
- **Core:** Solve pressing problems with unmatched performance
- **Financial:** Highlight ROI or cost savings
- **Operational:** Offer efficiency and integration ease

o **Strategic:** Focus on innovation and competitive positioning

o **Social:** Demonstrate ethical and societal impact

Step 4: Harmonizing Value and Needs

Align value propositions with customer archetypes to create synergy.

Step 5: Fine-Tuning for Success

Tailor your messaging for harmony and regularly revisit your CFOSS strategy. Are customer needs shifting? Are value propositions still resonating? Continuous refinement through feedback and data analysis helps keep your innovation engaging, adaptable, and impactful.

The CFOSS framework is not a static checklist but a dynamic guide, evolving alongside your innovation and the needs of your customers. This ongoing process of refinement helps your offerings stay relevant, appealing, and aligned with shifting market demands.

To see how this framework plays out in the real world, let's turn to the da Vinci Surgical System. Its adoption journey reveals how the CFOSS framework and the five steps of the Innovation Adoption Pathway can surface critical alignment gaps and guide strategic refinement over time.

Here's how the IAP can be applied to the robotic surgery case study, showcasing how Intuitive Surgical navigated CFOSS dimensions to accelerate adoption:

Step 1: Identify the Innovation

Innovation: The da Vinci Surgical System, a robotic-assisted surgery platform.

Problem it Solves: Enables minimally invasive surgery for complex procedures previously limited to open techniques, reducing recovery time, surgical trauma, and improving precision.

Step 2: Tuning Into Your Audience

<u>Core Customers – Surgeons</u>

Priority: Solve procedural pain points, improve surgical outcomes.

Behavior: Collaborated in refining instruments and procedures to optimize use.

Example: Dr. Menon and Dr. Feuer co-developed techniques and tools that transformed surgical standards.

Financial Customers – Hospital CFOs and Value Committees

Priority: Economic sustainability and ROI.

Behavior: Demanded cost modeling by DRG, analyzed per-case cost increases.

Example: CFOs highlighted concerns with routine laparoscopic cases being shifted to robotic, adding unnecessary cost.

Operational Customers – OR Directors, Surgical Teams

Priority: Workflow integration, training, resource utilization.

Behavior: Developed training matrices, optimized scheduling and inventory.

Example: Created systems for staff proficiency and minimized disruption to throughput.

Strategic Customers – Hospital Executives

Priority: Market leadership and competitive positioning.

Behavior: Acted quickly when market share or surgical talent was at risk.

Example: Hospitals like Florida Hospital and Saint Joseph's of Atlanta reinvested aggressively, recruiting top surgeons to secure strategic advantage.

Social Customers – Patient Advocates, NGOs

Priority: Equitable access, education, and quality-of-life outcomes.

Behavior: Informed patient decision-making, highlighted disparities, and advocated for underserved communities.

Example: The American Cancer Society and groups supporting Jehovah's Witnesses emphasized robotic surgery's alignment with patient values.

Step 3: Composing the Value Proposition

CVP: Enabled precision in complex surgeries, transforming practice and outcomes for frontline surgeons.

FVP: Showed long-term ROI through reduced hospital stays, premium reimbursements, and increased patient volumes.

OVP: Enhanced surgical throughput and optimized resource utilization through streamlined setup, reduced learning curves, and coordinated training strategies.

SVP: Offered hospitals competitive advantage by attracting elite talent and increasing market share.

SoVP: Aligned with community health goals, addressing disparities and offering inclusive care solutions.

Step 4: Harmonizing Value and Needs

Initial Misalignment: Early cardiothoracic adoption was hampered by complexity (Core), high costs (Financial), integration friction (Operational), unclear competitive ROI (Strategic), and initially unclear (Social).

Adjustment: Intuitive Surgical adapted its strategy by refining product features and redirecting clinical focus toward procedures where robotic advantages were most compelling namely, prostatectomy and complex hysterectomy. These shifts addressed the performance and outcome priorities of core customers. Simultaneously, the company introduced advanced financial models, improved training protocols, and tailored messaging to hospital administrators emphasizing patient demand trends, brand differentiation, and surgeon recruitment value. Over time, the social value proposition evolved as cancer advocacy groups and other patient organizations began informing their communities about robotic surgery options, expanding awareness without formally endorsing the technology. These combined efforts helped realign the innovation with each CFOSS archetype, turning early adoption barriers into scalable momentum.

Step 5: Fine-Tuning for Success

Continuous Feedback: As the da Vinci Surgical System expanded beyond early adopters, Intuitive Surgical consistently revisited its strategy to reflect shifting customer priorities. Feedback from surgeons influenced iterative improvements to instruments and interface design, reducing setup time and enhancing precision. Operational data from hospitals informed new tools for measuring throughput, cost efficiency, and OR utilization, leading to tailored onboarding programs that minimized workflow disruptions. Financial models were adapted based on insights from CFOs and value committees, emphasizing DRG-specific returns and risk-adjusted value cases. Meanwhile, input from social customers, including patient advocacy groups and public health organizations, prompted new efforts in education and outreach to ensure that messaging addressed equity, access, and awareness.

This feedback loop was reinforced by a growing body of clinical literature. In just the first quarter of 2008, 117 da Vinci-related clinical papers were published across multiple specialties. By 2014, that number had grown to over 7,000 peer-reviewed articles and more than 1,000 comparative studies. These studies not only validated use cases but also informed design, training, and communication strategies, creating a robust cycle of learning and adaptation.

In parallel, the progression of FDA approvals from initial general laparoscopic procedures to highly specialized applications in gynecology, pediatric surgery, and single-site hysterectomy reflected Intuitive's responsiveness to clinical feedback. Each regulatory milestone expanded the system's value across CFOSS domains, reinforcing its utility for core users, enhancing strategic differentiation, and enabling broader operational and social adoption.

Result: This sustained refinement process, shaped by direct user feedback, institutional data, regulatory evolution, and a growing body of evidence, transformed the da Vinci system into a scalable, industry-defining platform with strong buy-in across all CFOSS customer archetypes.

The IAP offers a structured way to align your solution with customer needs across CFOSS dimensions. But adoption rarely unfolds in a straight line. This next section offers a practical playbook of field-tested guidance to help you move from early interest to scalable growth. Whether you're just launching or working to refine your go-to-market strategy, these steps will help you put CFOSS into action, one customer at a time.

A Playbook for CFOSS-Driven Adoption

Early-stage innovation adoption is where the CFOSS framework truly earns its keep. This is the part of the journey where precision matters, resources are limited, and every interaction must count. The following playbook offers practical guidance on how to translate your CFOSS value propositions into tangible adoption momentum, step-

by-step. We'll walk through four critical stages:
- » Identifying the Right Entry Point
- » Establishing Your Beachhead
- » Beyond the Beach
- » Pushing Onward

Each builds on the last, starting with activating your closest allies, then leveraging their support to reach more pragmatic customers, and finally turning momentum into market movement.

Identifying the Right Entry Point

Before you can establish a beachhead, you need to identify the right place to land. In the context of innovation adoption, not all markets or customers, offer the same opportunity to build early traction. The goal is to find an entry point that supports short-term wins while laying the groundwork for long-term growth across CFOSS dimensions.

To illustrate this, we can look to a historic example that holds personal meaning for me as a West Point graduate and grandson of a World War II veteran. Consider Operation Overlord, better known as the Battle of Normandy. The Allies needed a strategic foothold to begin liberating France and, ultimately, Western Europe from Nazi control. But the challenge was immense. Hitler had charged Field Marshal Erwin Rommel with building the Atlantic Wall. It was a sprawling network of bunkers, mines, and fortifications stretching more than 240 miles and constructed with 17 million cubic tons of concrete and 1.2 million tons of steel. [66]

The Allies considered every stretch of shoreline, from Norway to the southern coast of France. The right beachhead had to meet several key criteria: it had to be less fortified than other sites, within range of air support, near a major port, and have terrain suitable for tank movement. Normandy emerged as the optimal choice. It wasn't perfect, but it was winnable, and more importantly, expandable.

Innovation adoption follows a similar logic. You may have multiple potential markets or customer segments, but not all are created equal. The trick is finding a place to start that supports both immediate traction and future scalability.

A strong entry point requires a mix of money, access, and pace. Ideally, early customers have the budget and authority to purchase, the proximity to engage in collaboration, and the urgency to act quickly. Few startups will find perfect conditions on all three fronts, but choosing an entry point with at least two of these traits often provides enough lift to launch the adoption journey.

Just as important is the alignment between your offering and the CFOSS dimensions of the initial problem being solved. A well-chosen entry point addresses an urgent and recognizable opportunity. Take the time to assess whether your offering creates multi-dimensional value. Are you addressing a problem worth solving?

A crucial component in early-stage adoption is alignment. Before Normandy, on August 19, 1942. The allies attempted an amphibious assault at Dieppe in Operation Jubilee. Despite the advantage of surprise, this operation was an overwhelming defeat, as almost 70% of the participating soldiers were either captured or killed. The difference is that the operation was fraught with misalignment. Poor coordination between sea and land units created landing bottlenecks. The landing points were poorly surveyed, and as a result, about half the tanks that made it to shore were stranded.[67] The lack of planning was evident in communication, coordination, support, and advancement efforts. The mission requirements were not aligned with the organizational action.

The adoption pathway needs to have the capital available to support market entry and expansion efforts. Initial resources may come in the form of investment capital but ultimately needs to include customers with budget and authority to purchase. In terms of access, the new venture or idea must have contact with key stakeholders, including buyers, end-users, and suppliers. If the innovation is cut off from key personnel, it will suffer. Lastly, the innovation pathway needs to exhibit urgency to push the purchasing process and product or service utilization.

Innovation adoption is about traction, and traction is a function of pace and adoption. It's not enough for the consumer market to adopt a new idea or process. The rate at which a startup captures capital and customers contributes to its ability to sustain market adoption. The goal isn't to build a beach house but to establish an entry point that supports market expansion.

The mixture of money, access, and pace varies, and the combination presents different opportunities and challenges. The best-case scenario is paying customers and capital funding, access to key stakeholders, and rhythmic growth. In the startup space, much attention is given to seeking capital from family and friends, angel investors, and venture capitalists. This is understandable as a well-funded business can invest in product development, build prototypes, and hire teams.

However, angel investors only invest in approximately 3 per every 100 deals.[68] In an article titled, '*Why 99.95% Of Entrepreneurs Should Stop Wasting Time Seeking Venture Capital*', Venture Capitals are reported to invest in only 1 of every 200 businesses ventures.[69] Making matters worse is the presence of investment inequity, from government funding sources, such as Small Business Innovation Research (SBIR) and Small Business Technology Transfer (STTR) programs to venture capital funding, female and minority founders experience even lower investment rates.[70;71;72]

This makes the arduous task of raising startup capital even more daunting for some founders. The odds of a high school baseball player making the pros are far better than a minority founder receiving funding.[73] There has to be a better beach. Starters may find a more realistic and advantageous approach to innovation adoption by pursuing access and a pace-oriented adoption plan.

Atlanta-based Spanx founder and CEO Sara Blakely took a different approach to innovation adoption. In 1998, she launched Spanx—the women's undergarment and hosiery brand—using $5,000 of her own savings and made the deliberate decision not to pursue outside investment. That choice came with challenges.

In the early days, she recounted how manufacturers responded to her cold calls:

"And you are...?"

"And you're with...?"

"And you're financially backed by...?"

At that point, they would politely decline: "Oh, it's so nice to meet you, Sara, but we're not interested. Have a nice day."

Her decision not to seek external funding initially limited her access to most hosiery manufacturers, many of whom were unwilling to take her seriously without a financial backer.[74]

But instead of spending her time pitching to investors or attending roadshows, Blakely focused on what she could control, pursuing customers. She hired a patent attorney but completed most of the application herself to reduce costs.[75] Rather than chase backing from hosiery mills that weren't giving her the time of day, she kept cold-calling until she found one that would. In the end, a manufacturer agreed thanks to the advice of his daughters. (Mine have been nudging me to finish this book for months.)

Through this hard-won access, Blakely made critical discoveries. She learned that sizing in the industry was based on plastic silhouettes, not real women. She uncovered that most brands used the same waistband across all sizes. And she realized the entire industry was operating without truly engaging their customers.

Too often, we focus on what we don't have instead of activating what we do. We overlook our Locus of Influence (LOI). The sphere in which we can access and influence customer and stakeholder behavior and decision-making. Think of it as a more actionable version of your personal network. You may have thousands of LinkedIn connections, but only a fraction are willing to take action when you ask.

Blakely worked with the access she had and activated her LOI. Through a friend who was a graphic designer, she developed mockups for product packaging. Like Blakely, entrepreneurs must begin by leveraging what's already within their LOI. Consider the Apollo 13 mission. When the astronauts faced a life-threatening crisis with compromised oxygen, electricity, and propulsion systems, mission control had to engineer a solution using only the materials available onboard.[76] In a similar spirit, Blakely focused on what she had: $5,000, a drive to start the patent process, sales experience, and the determination to visit hosiery mills. She wrote her own patent, contacted manufacturers directly, and designed the packaging herself.

After Nieman Marcus agreed to stock Spanx, Blakely activated her network, encouraging people across the country to purchase the product. She traveled store to store, personally pitching Spanx to customers, meeting with sales associates, and educating them on her creation.[77] She even rearranged product placement when necessary to increase visibility.

Her access-driven approach helped forge critical relationships with customers, suppliers, and distributors. These grassroots efforts paid off. Spanx grew into a global brand without spending a dollar on advertising for its first sixteen years.

Blakely's commitment to access shaped not only the purchasing process but also the product's utilization. It accelerated the pace of adoption. She didn't wait for others to act. She drove the process forward herself. Her direct engagement with stakeholders enabled rapid iteration. When she discovered that sizing was based on plastic silhouettes, she adapted. When she learned that the industry used a one-size-fits-all waistband, she turned that into a competitive advantage. This blend of pace and access created traction.

What makes an access- and pace-oriented approach so powerful is its ability to increase a founder's appeal to investors. Traction becomes tangible evidence of product-solution fit, product-market fit, and founder-market fit. It de-risks the venture, generates early revenue, and strengthens negotiating leverage. For investors, it passes what's often called the "distance traveled test." Venture capitalists are far more likely to invest in ventures that have already demonstrated momentum.

The distance traveled test evaluates what the founding team has accomplished with the resources available to them. In Blakely's case, it's a question of what she achieved with $5,000 and whether that progress would justify investing $100,000. No-brainer, right? By emphasizing access and pace over capital, she turned her savings into a product, a company, and eventually a global brand. In 2012, she became the youngest self-made female billionaire.

Reflecting on her journey, Blakely said, "I'm of the belief system for me in my journey to start small, think big, and scale fast."[78] That mindset captures the essence of CFOSS in early-stage innovation: making the most of what you have, staying close to your customers, and building momentum with intention. Identifying the entry point is just the beginning. The real work and the real opportunity begins when you land.

Establishing The Beachhead

Beachheads are not for the faint of heart. Most startups are short on resources and long on uncertainty. They're entering markets without a safety net, no brand recognition, limited credibility, and no traction to lean on.

That's why beachhead operations require allies. And there's no better partner than Problem Pioneers.

These core customers are often the first to believe in your innovation, not because of hype, but because of proximity. They're close to the problem you're solving. They've felt the friction, wrestled with the constraints, and recognize the value in a better way.

While Problem Pioneers help define the problem, Network Ambassadors can help deepen your understanding of who's most affected. They might not be the first users, but they bring powerful context

Finding the Right Allies

Start with the people and partners you can reach directly. Look for Problem Pioneers who are close to the problem and eager to solve it, and Network Ambassadors who care deeply about the community it impacts.

Your extended network may also hold allies. Consider industry peers, mission-aligned advocates, or early champions who recognize the importance of the problem even if they aren't affected directly. When your message is clear and your cause is shared, it's surprising how quickly new partnerships can form.

Building your beachhead isn't about making a splash. It's about forging early trust. Core customers give you the technical credibility to stand up your innovation. Social customers give it the moral and communal weight that helps others pay attention.

You'll need both perspectives, but it starts with Core.

Validating the CVP and SoVP with Core and Social Customers

Each stage of the innovation adoption pathway presents an opportunity to gain traction by validating specific value propositions. At the beachhead stage, the focus is on collaborating with your core and social customers to validate the CVP and SoVP. These are your "Shaka" customers. Those who share a sense of alignment and energy with your mission. When you work with them, it feels less like selling and more like teaming up for a shared cause.

Earlier, we identified potential core and social customers who are likely to champion your innovation. Now is the time to validate their alignment. At this point in the journey, there's often little financial reward. That's why identifying true Shaka customers, those who demonstrate both verbal enthusiasm and observable engagement, is essential. Beware of imposters. Their caution or pragmatism can dampen momentum.

Start by engaging these early believers in conversations about the problem space. Invite them to share their experiences and perspectives. Ask about what they've seen, what's been missing, and why it matters. Watch for genuine expressions of care for the problem, for the people affected, and for the outcomes your innovation hopes to create. These early dialogues help deepen your understanding of direct benefits while surfacing adjacent or indirect opportunities you may have missed.

One powerful way to capture their insights is to ask a simple question.

"If this solution truly worked, how would it impact your work or your world?"

Invite them to sketch it on a napkin. What you receive might be lists, doodles, or diagrams, but it's often more revealing than a slide deck. These informal reflections frequently uncover value your team didn't anticipate, especially in the social dimension.

Where possible, bring two or three core and social customers together. Whether in person or virtually, this small peer group discussion surfaces shared hopes, priorities, and tensions. It's a chance to hear their aspirations, not just for your product, but for the community and difficulties they care about. These conversations also help uncover social value you can't find in surveys or dashboards.

Some might call this customer discovery, and in part it is. But this is not a general-purpose exercise. It's purposeful validation with early allies, directed toward clarifying the CVP and SoVP. These early insights allow you to refine your CVP and SoVP.

You'll start to see how these two propositions connect to broader value domains. For instance, feedback on core features might reveal operational efficiencies you hadn't considered, or stories from social customers may highlight strategic relevance in ways that strengthen your position in the market. Just as different communities experience the same product differently, they also assign value in different ways.

Incorporate Lessons Learned

Shaka customers knowledge often surpasses your own when it comes to the problem landscape, stakeholder ecosystem, and competing solutions. In some cases, their networks become your next beachhead. Be sure to capture what systems and workflows they currently use. This insight helps you anticipate future integration points and navigate operational expectations down the line.

As you learn from these early partners, you'll find that some parts of your messaging truly connect, while others fall flat. Pay attention. It's not always obvious what motivates customers to act, especially when you're close to the product. Your collaboration with them should help clarify your CVP and SoVP.

After this phase, step back and reassess your CVP and SoVP messaging. Tighten it. Remove anything that misrepresents or muddies your core or social value. Refine your narrative until your value proposition is simple, clear, and actionable. In early adoption, traction often follows clarity. And clarity comes from listening well.

Conduct Access-Oriented Activities

At this point, you've done the foundational work. You've identified the right customers, clarified the Core and Social Value Propositions, explored the problem landscape, and validated your insights through collaboration. With those pieces in place, you're now ready for what many call The Ask.

But here's where entrepreneurs and innovators often misstep.

Some approach the wrong customer segment in the beachhead phase. Others overlook how environmental volatility or stakeholder uncertainty impacts adoption. Many accept customer enthusiasm at face value without validating both behavior and beliefs. And some forget to use feedback to refine the value propositions they're asking others to champion.

When these missteps are avoided, you're in a strong position to invite your early allies to help move adoption forward.

So what do you ask for?

You ask for access.

To advance beyond the beachhead, your goal is to secure access-oriented activities. The kind of commitments that only true Shaka customers can offer. For example, you might ask for introductions to other individuals or organizations that would benefit from your innovation. Or you might request that they recommend your offering to peers, managers, or decision-makers. You could invite them to participate in trials or pilot programs that showcase the core or social value of your solution.

You might also ask them to serve as references or to participate in open forums and roundtables about the problem your innovation addresses. Their credibility, proximity to the issue, and persistence to solve it make them powerful advocates in rooms you may not yet have access to.

Importantly, you're not asking Core and Social customers to make the purchase, at least not yet. Don't get me wrong if they offer to buy your solution, by all means, make the sale. But remember, traction doesn't come from a single transaction.

In an access- and pace-oriented approach, traction precedes transactions. Many Core and Social customers don't hold budget authority and that's okay. What they do hold is influence. Because they're close to the problem and deeply aligned with your CVP and SoVP, they're trusted voices to the decision-makers who come next. They can validate the need, elevate the urgency, and frame the potential.

The goal isn't to close a deal. It's to open a door. When Shaka customers lend their credibility and connections to your cause, they help accelerate your path to broader adoption.

Prepare for the Next Phase

Your beachhead operations set the stage for what comes next. The access-oriented activities you pursued with Problem Pioneers and Network Ambassadors helped build trust, credibility, and early traction. These activities also refined your Core and Social Value Propositions, laying the groundwork for strengthening your SVP.

Beyond the Beach

It's easy to get comfortable on the beach. After all, these customers get you. Conversations flow naturally. They care about the problem, resonate with your mission, and believe in the cause. These are your earliest and easiest allies. The ones who understand why you left your job, took the risk, and built something new.

But adoption doesn't happen on the beach.

To truly gain market foothold, you need to move beyond the early believers and into the realm of customers who are not thinking about belief but about competitive advantage. This is the next frontier.

The goal now is to harness the momentum you've built to reach the next tier of adopters. While the beachhead phase validated your Core and Social Value Propositions, this next phase focuses on testing your SVP. This phase moves beyond problem-solving and into creating tangible, strategic value. In other words, it's time to engage customers who are looking to win.

These are your Visionary Trailblazers who aren't satisfied with the status quo. They see innovation as a lever for strategic gain. They move fast, make bold decisions, and are energized by outperforming the market, their peers, or even their own past benchmarks.

To get off the beach, you'll need their urgency, their ambition, and their willingness to take calculated risks. You're no longer just proving that your idea works, we did this with the Problem Pioneers. You're demonstrating that it wins in the market. Visionary Trailblazers help you make that case by validating your product-market fit and confirming your SVP.

They are the launch pad for market movement.

Identify Early Adopters

Getting off the beach requires more than effort. It requires leverage. The traction built with Shaka customers, especially core, isn't just validation; it's a springboard. As you move toward Visionary Trailblazers, you're not starting from zero. You're building from momentum.

In the beachhead phase, your LOI guided your outreach. Now, it's time to extend that influence by tapping into your Shaka customers' LOI. Why? Because an introduction from a core and social customers carries weight. You may not have direct access to the Visionary Trailblazer, but your Network Ambassador does, and their credibility opens doors.

When a trusted Problem Pioneer introduces your offering, it is more than a handoff. It becomes an endorsement. Even before you speak, your CVP and SVP are already being validated. In essence, the core customer is saying, "This is something you should pay attention to."

That kind of access accelerates pace. And pace is critical here. In this phase, you're not trying to cold-pitch a stranger. You're stepping into a warm introduction backed by real-world insight and shared context.

This doesn't mean your own LOI is irrelevant. Continue to engage your direct and extended network. But recognize that high-profile targets (like getting your book into Oprah's hands) can drain time and energy without guaranteed return. It's tempting to chase big wins, but sustainable adoption favors steady, strategic movement.

Momentum matters. Instead of stalling your efforts to reach unreachable targets, follow the path of access and urgency. Let your Problem Pioneers and Network Ambassadors guide the way toward strategic customers who are primed to push your innovation further.

Conducting SVP Validating Activities

In the CFOSS hand model, remember the SVP is represented by the ring finger. It signifies a longer-term relationship grounded in shared goals and mutual benefit.

When my wife and I were dating, we discovered a shared love for Akitas. That common interest sparked more frequent conversations, tighter schedules, and intentional effort to stay connected; classic signs of growing alignment. The same dynamics apply when validating strategic value with early customers: shared goals, increasing engagement, and a quickening pace are indicators that you're on the right track.

As Mike Tomlin, head coach of the Pittsburgh Steelers, once said, "We can't do this with hostages. We need volunteers." That wisdom applies here. We're not looking for customers who are reluctantly along for the ride. We want willing partners; customers who see this innovation as a path to strategic gain.

Just like in the previous phase, we must validate that our assumptions about customer types are accurate. We don't want to misdiagnosis CFOSS customer archetypes. Misdiagnosis here can stall momentum. If we start solving for scale before the offering has gained early traction, we risk derailing our growth. That's why behavioral and verbal confirmation is essential. The goal is not to find customers who are always early adopters. It's to find customers who are early adopters for this innovation.

What SVP Validation Looks Like

These validation activities involve candid, collaborative discussions with Visionary Trailblazers. We explore how the innovation could enhance their strategic positioning. We listen for urgency. Are they seeking to be first to market? Do they want to outpace competitors? Are they focused on elevating their brand? Their answers help us determine whether our SVP truly resonates with their organizational goals.

Ask what other initiatives they've implemented to gain an edge in this area. If they've tried something before, how did it go? Where did it fall short? These reflections provide insight into how your offering aligns with or strengthens their current strategies.

Frame your innovation as a convergence of value streams. Reference the validation you've already received from Problem Pioneers. Show how your offering links the Core and Social Value Propositions to longer-term strategic objectives. This builds a compelling narrative that the innovation isn't just solving a problem. It's helping shape a more competitive future.

Strategic customers don't move slowly. When they believe in the strategic upside, they act decisively with their focus, time, and budgets.

Share Urgency, Not Just Strategy

Aligning with strategic customers requires more than business cases. It requires shared urgency. Founders and Visionary Trailblazers are often racing toward the same goal. They just approach it from different angles. For the founder, traction is oxygen. For the Visionary Trailblazers innovation is a route to gain.

This mutual urgency can strengthen trust. It sharpens communication and increases the frequency and pace of engagement. And it helps create traction not just in sentiment, but in strategic motion.

Tailor Your Interactions

While your work with Problem Pioneers may have emphasized collaboration and co-creation, Visionary Trailblazers may introduce new dynamics. In highly competitive markets, they may ask for exclusivity over a region or time window. That's not always the case and context matters. During COVID, for example, hospitals that typically competed intensely chose to collaborate to fight a common threat.

The key is to understand that strategic customers are motivated by positional gain. Your interactions should reflect an appreciation for that. Speak to competitive advantages. Reference the momentum already achieved. And show how your innovation positions them to win now and into the future.

Incorporate Lessons Learned

There's a distinct kind of learning that comes from engaging with Visionary Trailblazers. It's learning that goes beyond what we gleaned from our Problem Pioneers. These are customers who view innovation through a strategic lens. Their focus isn't just on whether your solution works, but on whether it can advance their position in the market. Each conversation offers insight into what competitive advantage truly means for different decision-makers.

As you move from one strategic customer to the next, you begin to recognize patterns. What do these Trailblazers consistently prioritize? Where do they see the most value? What concerns do they raise? These observations help you not only refine your SVP but also understand how to configure your value streams in ways that reinforce and amplify each other.

Visionary Trailblazers are also forward-thinking but calculated. They want innovation, but not at the expense of performance, reputation, or operational integrity. Their feedback helps you shape a multi-dimensional value proposition that balances innovation with reliability.

You'll also learn a lot about sales cycle dynamics. Strategic customers don't move slowly, but they do move with purpose. Their urgency, rooted in a desire to outperform, reveals what it really takes to accelerate adoption. Before working with one such customer, I didn't realize a hospital could make a multi-million-dollar purchasing decision in less than 90 days. But with a clear SVP and the right internal alignment, they moved fast because the value was clear and the gain was strategic.

Visionary Trailblazers also provide real-world insight into pricing thresholds, implementation expectations, and the pace required to transition from promise to purchase. In the early days of robotic surgery, for example, the core benefit lay in converting complex open procedures to minimally invasive approaches. Much of the momentum behind this transition came from strategic-minded surgeons and administrators—true Visionary Trailblazers—who recognized the competitive advantage of leading with innovation. Intuitive Surgical acknowledged this connection:

"We believe these efforts will benefit early-adopting hospitals by increasing their market share in the procedures and specialties that benefit from Intuitive surgery."[79]

After working with these customers, revisit your SVP. Clarify the strategic advantages it delivers. Eliminate any messaging that overpromises or underdelivers. Prioritize the aspects of your offering that support their goals and match their urgency.

Conduct Pace-Oriented Activities

At this point, you've identified your Visionary Trailblazers, validated your SVP, and refined it through meaningful collaboration. Now comes the ask. In this phase, the ask is pace.

Getting off the beach requires momentum, and pace is what Visionary Trailblazers thrive on. These are the customers with urgency in their DNA. They're not looking to be convinced they're looking to win. What you're offering is a chance to do just that. So ask them to act.

Specifically, you're asking them to purchase your offering in a short period of time. These early transactions generate revenue, but more importantly, they create motion. Because Visionary Trailblazers move fast, their purchases can influence others to follow suit. Their early commitment signals market viability and in many cases, it prompts hesitant peers to take action.

You also want to encourage them to publicize their success. Strategic customers don't just want to win quietly. They want to lead visibly. Visibility reinforces credibility and credibility fuels adoption.

Importantly, Visionary Trailblazers are not investing in your offering as a science project. That's the mindset of a Problem Pioneer. Visionary Trailblazers are investing in their own strategic outcomes. They expect a return, not just once, but over time. That's what makes them powerful partners. As we discussed before, they're reinvestors.

Because they're among the first to see how your solution plays out in real-world settings, they're also first to uncover complementary offerings, add-on benefits, or future revenue streams. Their foresight makes them valuable collaborators.

Their real-world insights extend across the CFOSS spectrum. With their early experiences, they've already helped shape your CVP and SoVP. Now, their ongoing adoption journey allows you to sharpen your FVP and OVP, adding depth to your business model and preparing your offering for broader adoption.

Prepare for the Next Phase

Access helped you establish your beachhead. Pace got you off of it. But now comes the challenge of building on that momentum without losing ground.

The next phase requires consolidation, solidifying your progress so far and setting the stage for wider market adoption. A great place to start is by celebrating the wins of your earliest customers. Showcase how Visionary Trailblazers and Problem Pioneers have experienced success across the Core, Social, and Strategic value dimensions. Share their stories through blog posts, videos, conference talks, and social media.

Peer-to-peer credibility is one of your most powerful growth levers. When a new customer hears directly from someone who's already made the leap and even better, reinvested, it accelerates trust. Customers who've purchased multiple times often make the best advocates when speaking to someone still considering their first.

To keep up your pace, you'll need to ensure easy access to references and stories. Build a system where those conversations happen quickly and naturally. And don't just collect testimonials, spotlight reinvestments. They're tangible proof that your offering isn't just promising, it's performing.

This is also a good time to refine your remaining value propositions. Visionary Trailblazers who've been through multiple adoption cycles offer critical feedback about implementation, integration, and ongoing use. Leveraging their insights to sharpen your FVP and OVP so that your offering is even stronger before approaching the Fiscal Architects and Productivity Gurus.

You're no longer purely building momentum. You're preparing for scale.

Pushing Onward

The adoption journey began on the beach, gained momentum inland, and now reaches toward what we hope is the first of many summits. The objective of this phase is to crest the Early Majority hill. It's not a finish line, but a crucial milestone on the path to sustainable innovation adoption.

Up to this point, Problem Pioneers, Network Ambassadors and Visionary Trailblazers have been instrumental in validating your Core, Social, and Strategic Value Propositions. Their belief, urgency, and willingness to act gave your innovation its first push. But now, the focus shifts. The next group of customers isn't motivated by belief or vision. They are motivated by proof.

This next phase is about staying power. They're not looking to be first. They're looking to be confident. Their involvement marks a pivotal shift from testing your offering to scaling it.

Financial and operational customers are deliberate and discerning. They're not energized by novelty but by practicality. They demand that innovation be dependable, sustainable, and financially sound. When they buy in, it's more than validation. It's stabilization. These customers are the foundation on which *lasting* adoption is built.

Identify Early Majority Customers

Unlike previous phases, you won't be relying on previous customers to introduce you to this next group. There's a good reason for that. Visionary Trailblazers have made significant investments in your offering, some even repeatedly. They've done so to create strategic advantage. Asking them to connect you with their competitors can unintentionally shorten the runway of that advantage, and in doing so, may strain the relationship.

That's why this next move requires finesse.

The Early Majority doesn't look for innovation cues in market saturation. They're not waiting for 100 customers. They're watching for the right ones. For them, it's not how many have adopted; it's who adopted. Familiarity breeds comfort, and trust comes from proximity. These customers need to know someone they recognize and respect has already made the leap.

Think back to the rise of Spanx. In 2000, Oprah Winfrey named it one of her favorite products of the year.[80] That single endorsement moved the needle not because of how many people had adopted Spanx, but because Oprah had. To these customers the source of validation matters as much as the message.

You don't need to rely on a direct introduction to gain this kind of traction. Instead, leverage the public credibility that your Shaka customers and Trailblazers have built. Their visibility (i.e. their speaking engagements, media coverage, blog posts, case studies, and word-of-mouth recommendations) creates the trust bridge that financial and operational customers walk across.

Study the locus of influence of your existing customers. Which communities know and trust them? Which peers value their opinion? That's where your Harmonizing customers (financial and operational—the fingers) are waiting. You don't need to change your message. You simply need to amplify the messenger.

Conduct FVP and OVP Validating Activities

Harmonizing customers, financial and operational, determine whether your innovation can truly scale. In the CFOSS hand model, they represent the peace sign: a balance of performance and practicality. Their priorities center on financial viability and operational fit.

By this phase, your FVP has likely matured. Early-stage versions carried higher production costs and were subject to frequent iteration. Now, with feedback from Problem Pioneers and Visionary Trailblazers in hand, you've streamlined delivery, clarified pricing, and built a stronger economic case. Testimonials from those early adopters provide added proof that your offering delivers real value.

Still, a strong FVP only gets you part of the way.

Harmonizing customers live at the intersection of systems, staff, and execution. The OVP is just as critical. These customers aren't averse to change, but they demand that it integrate seamlessly into their existing environment. Implementation can't cause disruption.

This is where peer validation becomes essential.

Create opportunities for prospects to speak directly with current users, especially those with similar roles or system constraints. These conversations build confidence. When a fellow operator explains how they navigated onboarding, overcame initial friction, or integrated the solution into a complex workflow, uncertainty gives way to trust.

Often, these discussions surface operational issues your prospects hadn't even considered along with practical solutions your earlier customers have already deployed. These experiences show that your innovation doesn't just work; it works here, in environments like theirs.

Also remember these customers rarely act alone. Purchasing decisions typically involve committees, procurement teams, and operational leads. This isn't resistance. It's risk management. Your job is to equip each stakeholder group with what they need to say yes.

One final hurdle is compatibility. Will this solution work with our current systems? Will it slow us down? To address those questions, highlight where your offering has already been successfully deployed. Share case studies, usage data, or connect them directly with peers in similar contexts. Show them, don't just tell them, that implementation is achievable.

In short, this phase isn't about bold promises. It's about proving reliability. When you demonstrate that your innovation can align with their budgets and their workflows, you give Harmonizing customers the assurance they need to move forward.

Incorporate Lessons Learned

At the end of this phase, every CFOSS value proposition comes into focus. What it takes to establish a beachhead is different from what's needed to get off the beach. And getting off the beach requires something else entirely from what's required to reach the summit. Each part of the innovation adoption journey demands new strategies and delivers new insights.

Up to this point, we've used access and pace to generate revenue. That's very different from leading with money to buy access or speed. You can see the difference in comparative company valuations. Founders who reach this phase may choose to pursue outside funding but now they're doing so with traction, customers, and a working revenue model.

As you consolidate what you've learned, take time to refine your CFOSS story. Add clarity where needed. Remove anything that no longer rings true. And adjust your messaging to reflect not just early adopters' priorities, but the broader industry's as well. The mountain is in sight.

Conduct Traction-Oriented Activities

Traction is what keeps progress from slipping. Like tires gripping the road, it's how you move forward without losing what you've already gained.

Gaining traction at the industry level requires more than just acquiring new customers. It demands that you retain them. This is the phase where adoption becomes sustainable. You've built momentum. Now, you need staying power.

To maintain and expand that traction, begin benchmarking your CFOSS value propositions against the status quo. Measure your innovation's performance compared to the industry standard. Demonstrate how your offering performs better, scales faster, or delivers more value. This helps convert the next wave of customers and solidifies your place in the market.

This is the time for third-party studies, case analyses, and white papers. Highlight metrics that show progress like growth rates, market share, customer satisfaction, and retention. When possible, show longitudinal impact: how your offering performs not just today, but over time.

These traction-oriented activities signal to the market that your innovation isn't just gaining ground but that it's built to stay. You're not just another entrant. You're becoming a major player. And that momentum sets the stage for whatever comes next.

From Traction to Transformation

From identifying your entry point to securing early traction, you've done more than prove your offering works. You've built a foundation for growth grounded in real customer insight, tested value propositions, and collaborative relationships. CFOSS guided you through the initial fog of uncertainty with precision, pace, and purpose.

But this is only the beginning.

What starts as a playbook for early-stage adoption evolves into a strategic lens for long-term success. The same CFOSS principles that helped you secure your first wins can now be applied across your entire organization from product development and segmentation to customer experience and business modeling. The next section explores how to unlock the broader potential of CFOSS and embed its mindset into the heart of how you operate and grow.

Unlocking the Broader Potential of CFOSS

The CFOSS framework offers a lens that can guide decision-making across your entire organization. When applied holistically, CFOSS reshapes how businesses innovate, connect with customers, and respond to changing market conditions. Below are several compelling use cases that illustrate its broader potential.

Product Development: Crafting Multi-dimensional Solutions

CFOSS serves as a blueprint for developing products that create value across multiple dimensions:

- » Core: Does your product solve meaningful problems with innovative precision?
- » Financial: Does it deliver measurable ROI or cost savings?
- » Operational: How easily does it integrate into existing workflows to improve efficiency?
- » Strategic: Will it help customers strengthen their market position or pursue new opportunities?
- » Social: Does it reflect societal priorities such as ethical responsibility?

By embedding CFOSS into the product development process, businesses can create offerings that meet the needs of diverse stakeholders and deliver enduring value.

How can you apply the CFOSS framework to improve your organizations approach to customer adoption?

Market Segmentation: Gaining a More Comprehensive Understanding of Customers

CFOSS offers a more dynamic lens for market segmentation, moving beyond surface-level demographics to focus on customer priorities across key value dimensions:

- » Cost-conscious buyers prioritize financial efficiency and long-term value.

» Efficiency-driven customers focus on seamless integration and productivity gains.
» Socially motivated consumers seek solutions that reflect ethical standards and community impact.

This approach supports more targeted messaging, tailored offerings, and smarter resource allocation, making it easier to meet the specific needs of each customer group.

Customer Journey Mapping: Personalizing the Experience

The CFOSS framework offers a powerful way to enhance each stage of the customer journey, not by adding more noise, but by focusing on what matters most to different types of customers:

» Early Interest: Highlight what solves their most pressing problem (Core), whether that's a performance breakthrough, a practical fix, or a faster way to get results.
» Evaluation: For some, that means financial justification. For others, it's seeing how easily the solution fits into their day-to-day workflows or how it advances a bigger strategic goal.
» Commitment and Onboarding: Operational customers look for clarity on training, implementation, and support. Tailoring these moments helps reduce friction and speed adoption.
» Ongoing Engagement: Social customers may expect to see long-term outcomes beyond their own experience. Providing evidence of shared benefit builds credibility and trust.

Business Modeling: Designing Strategy Around Customer Value

CFOSS can serve as a powerful design tool for shaping business models that deliver value across diverse stakeholder priorities. Rather than focusing on isolated functions, this approach ensures that strategy, operations, and customer experience are built with multi-dimensional alignment in mind:

» Customer Segments: Map your customer base using CFOSS archetypes. Distinguish between core problem-solvers, financial evaluators, operational users, strategic influencers, and social advocates to clarify who you're serving and what each group values.
» Value Propositions: Embed CFOSS thinking into how you define and communicate value. Design offerings that solve urgent challenges, deliver ROI, integrate smoothly, offer market

differentiation, and contribute to broader societal goals.
- » Channels and Relationships: Tailor your outreach and engagement strategies based on CFOSS profiles. Operational customers may prefer analytical white papers, while social customers may engage through community awareness or education campaigns.
- » Revenue Streams and Cost Structure: Build pricing and investment models that reflect value across dimensions. Consider flexible pricing, long-term ROI, and sustainable cost structures that support continued delivery of CFOSS value.
- » Key Resources, Activities, and Partnerships: Align internal capabilities and external partnerships with the delivery of CFOSS value. This may include R&D for core performance, training programs for operational integration, or collaborations with advocacy groups to scale social outreach

CFOSS helps organizations move beyond product-market fit and toward business-model resonance. When every element of the model supports multi-dimensional customer needs, companies gain the clarity and agility to grow with purpose.

The CFOSS framework is not just a methodology; it's a mindset. It invites companies to see themselves not as sellers of products but as partners in their customers' journeys toward greater success and impact.

Conclusion: The CFOSS Journey Beyond the Start Line

Navigating the early stages of customer adoption is both a challenge and an opportunity. As explored throughout this book, the CFOSS framework is more than a guide to product-market fit. It's a strategic approach for fostering sustained growth and building meaningful connections with customers.

The common hurdles of startups, including lengthy sales cycles, arduous negotiations, and constant uncertainty around customer acquisition, can be reimagined through the lens of CFOSS. When core, financial, operational, strategic, and social priorities are integrated, your innovation isn't merely introduced to the market. It is positioned with intention, precision, and the potential to make a difference.

Each chapter of this book has provided actionable insights to help structure value propositions and align them with customer archetypes, bridging the gap between the promise of innovation and the realities of adoption. CFOSS equips you with a framework to create long-term relationships and evolve alongside the needs of your customers.

CFOSS: A Strategy for Continuous Growth

The true strength of CFOSS lies in its adaptability. As markets evolve and customer expectations shift, the framework provides a road map to remain ahead of change. Innovation adoption becomes less of a gamble and more of a calculated strategy. One that can be revisited, refined, and recalibrated to meet new challenges and opportunities.

While the five-step CFOSS process is easy to implement, its real value emerges when CFOSS principles become ingrained in your organizational culture. Whether you are refining products, entering new markets, or optimizing internal processes, CFOSS helps you stay agile and aligned in a rapidly shifting world.

Thank you for joining us on this journey. We look forward to seeing how you apply CFOSS to redefine success in the innovation adoption race. Together, let's create solutions that truly matter.

Stay connected for additional resources, workshops, and tools to support your CFOSS journey. The race to early adoption is only the beginning.

CHAPTER 6 IN REVIEW

» The CFOSS framework integrates core, financial, operational, strategic, and social dimensions to craft resonant value propositions that foster deep customer connections and market impact.

» **Five-Step CFOSS Guide**: A structured process supports innovation adoption and alignment:
  o Identifying the innovation: Define your innovation through a CFOSS lens, addressing diverse customer priorities.
  o Tuning into your audience: Segment customer archetypes by CFOSS dimensions to refine messaging.
  o Composing the value proposition: Tailor targeted propositions across CFOSS pillars for maximum resonance.
  o Harmonizing value and needs: Align customer priorities with relevant value propositions to drive synergy.
  o Fine-tuning for success: Continuously adjust strategies based on customer feedback and evolving market dynamics.

» The CFOSS-Driven Adoption Playbook outlines four practical stages to build real traction in early markets:
  o Identifying the Right Entry Point: Find a market with urgency, access, and budget fit.
  o Establishing Your Beachhead: Collaborate with Core and Social customers to validate your CVP and SoVP.
  o Beyond the Beach: Engage Visionary Trailblazers to test and refine your Strategic Value Proposition.
  o Pushing Onward: Reach Financial and Operational customers by proving fit, reliability, and ROI at scale.

» The playbook emphasizes that adoption is not linear—traction is earned through clarity, access, pace, and real-world validation

AFTERWORD

The CFOSS® Journey: A Final Note

Here we are, at the end of this journey, or perhaps the beginning of yours. Together, we've explored customer archetypes, value propositions, the CFOSS framework, and even cautionary tales of startups that succeeded or stumbled. As you prepare to dive back into the trenches, let me leave you with one final thought. Innovation thrives on connection.

Throughout my career in entrepreneurship and innovation, I've seen a recurring pattern. Talented founders with brilliant ideas getting stuck, not for lack of drive or creativity, but because they were focusing on the wrong things. I've been there too. Caught in the endless cycle of perfecting, and delaying the crucial step of engaging with customers. Each delay sacrifices time, momentum, and invaluable opportunities to learn, adapt, and grow.

One founder shared with me how he perfected his product through countless internal iterations before unveiling it to the world. My immediate thought was, What about all the missed opportunities to learn from customers and refine the product based on their feedback? The CFOSS framework is designed to help you avoid this trap. It's about building *with* your customers, not just *for* them thereby creating value that resonates because it reflects their real needs and priorities.

So here's my advice. Start now. Share your ideas, your progress, and your vision with your customers early, often, and authentically. Treat them as partners in your innovation journey. The value of what you're building is more than the product itself. It's the relationships, trust, and community you create along the way.

The startup journey can be challenging, but it doesn't have to be lonely. Engage, listen, and collaborate. And you'll find that the path to success is not only achievable but also deeply rewarding.

Thank you for taking this journey with me. Now it's your turn to create something extraordinary. Go build, connect, and innovate with your customers by your side.

APPENDIX A: LESSONS FROM ROBOTIC SURGERY (CFOSS® CUSTOMERS)

The Core Customer Perspective

In the late 1990s, a group of visionary surgeons confronted a significant challenge. Despite decades of progress in surgical techniques, certain procedures remained resistant to minimally invasive approaches. Dr. Randall Chitwood, observing his cardiac patients endure painful recoveries following traditional sternotomies, envisioned a better solution.[81] Similarly, Dr. Mani Menon, grappling with the quality-of-life impacts for prostate cancer patients undergoing radical prostatectomies, sought transformative answers to these surgical challenges.[82]

The limitations of traditional laparoscopy had become glaringly apparent. The approach revolutionized procedures like cholecystectomy but fell short when applied to more complex surgeries. Rigid instruments, counterintuitive movements, and limited visualization made intricate dissection in confined spaces nearly impossible. Recognizing these shortcomings, core customer surgeons didn't merely highlight the problems. They dedicated themselves to finding solutions.

When the early da Vinci Surgical System was introduced, these core customers saw beyond its initial limitations to its transformative potential. Regularly meeting with representatives from Intuitive Surgical, they meticulously documented procedural challenges, offering detailed feedback to refine the system. Comments like "We need the wrist to rotate another fifteen degrees" or "The patient cart needs greater mobility for different approach angles" underscored their precise understanding of what the technology needed to succeed.

Dr. Menon's team at the Vattikuti Urology Institute rebuilt their operating rooms (ORs) around the da Vinci system, rigorously experimenting with patient positioning and port placement to optimize prostatectomy techniques. They tracked outcomes, documented results, and refined processes, creating a road map for broader adoption.

Similarly, Dr. Gerald Feuer collaborated with Intuitive Surgical to develop specialized instruments, using detailed sketches to demonstrate the precise movements required for complex oncologic gynecologic procedures like vaginal cuff closure. These collaborations spurred innovations such as EndoWrist instruments and fourth-arm functionality, transforming the robot into a versatile surgical tool.

These surgeons exemplified core customer behaviors, acting as individuals embedded in the development process who often participated in clinical trials and helped refine procedural techniques. Their contributions extended beyond merely adopting the technology. They actively shaped its evolution.

Even when challenges arose, core customers remained committed. Statements from early-adopting hospitals acknowledging "a few challenges with the new systems" reflected a willingness to persevere through growing pains. This commitment empowered a generation of innovative surgeons to co-create an industry.

The influence of these core customers reached far beyond their own practices. Their outcomes reduced blood loss, shorter hospital stays, and improved functional results provided the evidence necessary for broader market adoption Their engagement with engineering, procedural training, and clinical applications transformed robotic surgery from a novel innovation into an essential surgical tool.

As Intuitive Surgical noted in their 2004 report, "We believe these efforts will benefit early-adopting hospitals by increasing their market share in the procedures and specialties that benefit from Intuitive surgery."[83] These core customers went beyond purchasing the technology. They refined it, proving its value and laying the groundwork for widespread acceptance.

The Financial Customer Perspective

Surgeons envisioned clinical possibilities, as hospital CFOs and financial teams grappled with the complex economic realities that would determine whether robotic surgery could evolve from a promising innovation into a sustainable program.

Hospital CFOs approached robotic surgery by dissecting every cost component, including:
» Capital equipment costs per system
» Annual service contracts
» Disposable instrument costs per case
» Staff training requirements and associated productivity impacts
» Marketing investments needed to build program awareness

» Facility modifications for optimal system placement

These decision-makers exhibited behaviors emblematic of financial customers. When presented with the clinical potential of robotic surgery, their immediate response was, "Great, but let's look at the numbers." They meticulously analyzed procedure costs by DRG and ICD-9 codes, seeking to understand revenue implications across various surgical specialties. Their financial models compared robotic approaches with traditional and laparoscopic methods, factoring in:

» Reimbursement rates by procedure type
» Operating room time differentials
» Length of stay variations
» Supply chain impacts
» Staff utilization changes

Adding to this scrutiny, Value Analysis Committees and materials managers raised pointed questions. As one materials director noted, "The clinical benefits look promising, but at these costs, we need concrete evidence of economic sustainability." This sentiment reflected the characteristic risk assessment behaviors of financial customers, particularly in addressing:

» High fixed costs in a volatile healthcare market
» Uncertain procedure volumes during program development
» Complex training requirements impacting productivity
» Limited reimbursement premiums for robotic procedures

The financial analysis often exposed challenging economics. For example, reduced length of stay offered clear savings for complex procedures like prostatectomy; however, converting routine laparoscopic cases to robotics introduced cost pressures without delivering comparable clinical benefits. As one CFO observed, "We're seeing a cost increase per case for procedures that already had good outcomes."

This focus on measurable returns and sustainable economics created necessary tension in the adoption process. The rigorous analysis of financial customers on occasion delayed or limited program expansion, but it also ensured organizations developed realistic implementation strategies. This dynamic perfectly illustrated the influence of financial customers' behavior patterns, including detailed cost modeling, risk-focused questioning, and demands for tangible economic evidence in validating the foundations of innovation.

Through their analytical lens, financial customers helped transform robotic surgery from an exciting clinical innovation into a sustainable hospital program. Financial customers' insistence on economic viability was sometimes seen as overly conservative, but it ultimately shaped thoughtful and enduring adoption strategies.

The Operational Customer Perspective

The implementation of robotic surgery programs vividly illustrates how operational customers navigate the complexities of organizational change. Financial customers concentrated on costs, core customers championed clinical possibilities, and operational customers tackled the intricate challenge of integrating robotic surgery into existing surgical workflows.

Operational customers were particularly focused on the logistics of training entire surgical teams. Financial customers calculated the costs of training. At the same time, operational customers tackled questions such as: How do we maintain OR efficiency during staff training? What impact do parallel training sessions have on our schedule? They understood that the learning curve extended beyond surgeons to include nurses, surgical technicians, and anesthesia staff.[84]

Process mapping revealed significant coordination challenges, as training schedules had to accommodate both individual learning needs and the development of team cohesion. As one OR director remarked, "It's not enough to have trained individuals. We need cohesive teams that can work efficiently together." This led to the creation of comprehensive training matrices that tracked proficiency levels for individuals and teams alike, allowing the entire surgical unit to operate effectively under new protocols.

OR efficiency became a central concern for operational customers. They meticulously documented how robotic procedures affected room turnover times, procedure durations, and overall daily throughput. Using Gantt charts and process flows, they highlighted potential bottlenecks and resource conflicts that might not have been immediately apparent to other stakeholders.

The introduction of robotic systems also required a reevaluation of existing resources. As one materials manager explained, "We're not just adding new instruments. We're potentially disrupting the utilization patterns of our existing inventory." To address this, operational customers devised inventory management strategies that balanced maintaining traditional surgical capabilities with building robotic capacity.

As robotic surgery programs expanded from single surgeons to multiple users, operational customers faced the growing complexity of scaling operations. They identified exponential challenges in scheduling, resource allocation, and team coordination that arose as programs grew from one surgeon to many or from a single specialty to multiple services.

Through process analysis, they determined how network effects could either enhance or hinder operational efficiency. Increased usage helped justify the technology's costs but also amplified coordination challenges. Operational customers developed advanced scheduling systems and resource allocation protocols to manage these demands, so growth wouldn't compromise operational effectiveness.

The ripple effects of robotic surgery extended well beyond the OR. Operational customers mapped out how new surgical approaches influenced downstream departments, such as how reduced length of stay affected bed availability, staffing patterns, and discharge protocols. Their systems thinking approach allowed them to address these changes proactively, preventing bottlenecks in other parts of the hospital.

By meticulously documenting workflows and refining processes, operational customers transformed robotic surgery from an exciting technological advancement into a sustainable program. Their emphasis on workflow integration, resource optimization, and scalable systems was essential for successful implementation. Their cautious approach, though sometimes seen as overly methodical, ultimately prevented costly failures and enabled the sustainable growth of robotic surgery programs.

The Strategic Customer Perspective

The evolution of robotic surgery illustrates how strategic customers respond to competitive pressures with remarkable urgency, especially when market leadership positions are at stake. This urgency manifests at both institutional (B2B) and individual (B2C) levels, often driven by the threat of losing key surgical talent or market share to competitors.

Consider the case of a hospital executive who implemented a robotic surgery program in six weeks, a timeline typically considered impossibly aggressive for a capital investment of this scale. This decision was driven by two pressing threats. The first was the risk of losing surgical talent to competitors, and the second was declining patient volumes as consumers sought robotic surgery options elsewhere. This example highlights how strategic customers are willing to make bold, high-stakes moves when faced with clear competitive disadvantages.

Historical data from Intuitive Surgical's annual reports further illustrate this dynamic. In the early 2010s, the CEO of Ford Health System noted that their robotic program drove "double-digit increases in prostate cases." [85] Similarly, Florida Hospital's recruitment of Dr. Vip Patel and his team, who had completed more than two thousand robotic cases, resulted in significant market share gains.[86] Strategic customers understood that the initial $1.6 million to $2.5 million investment[87] in a robotic system could easily be justified by the retention or recruitment of a single high-volume surgeon, whose practice might generate $5 million to $10 million in annual revenue.

Today's financial metrics may have evolved, but the fundamental strategic calculation remains the same: evaluating capital investment against potential revenue loss from surgeon departures or market share erosion. For updated figures, readers can refer to Intuitive Surgical's most recent annual reports and SEC filings. However, the principles guiding these decisions continue to inform strategic customer behavior in healthcare.

Strategic customers' decision-making often centered on three key considerations:

» Surgeon retention and recruitment impact
» Market share protection and growth potential
» Long-term program development opportunities

These factors help explain why hospitals like Saint Joseph's of Atlanta aggressively pursued becoming "A World Leader in Robotic Surgery"[88] and why Florida Hospital evolved from acquiring their first robotic system in 2004 to establishing the Global Robotic Institute.[89] Their investments were not solely reactions to immediate competitive threats but strategic efforts to secure sustainable market leadership.

The pattern of reinvestment among strategic customers underscores their commitment. Between 2007 and 2011, repeat system sales increased dramatically, from 35 systems to 352.[90] These were not replacements but strategic expansions of robotic programs as hospitals sought to solidify their market positions.

Strategic customers also recognized the critical importance of the learning curve in robotic surgery. Studies suggested that surgeons required 150–250 procedures for proficiency and 1,000–1,500 cases for true mastery.[91][92] Early adopters gained a significant advantage in developing surgical expertise. Hospitals delaying implementation risked falling years behind in cultivating the necessary talent. For example, Dr. Sudhir Srivastava, after performing more than eight hundred robotic cardiac procedures in Odessa, Texas, was recruited to the University of Chicago Medical Center, underscoring the competitive dynamics in attracting experienced surgeons.[93]

The recruitment of Dr. Vip Patel by Florida Hospital exemplifies this comprehensive approach. Dr. Patel's recruitment extended beyond the individual surgeon to include members of his entire experienced team, demonstrating that strategic customers viewed robotic surgery not as a technology acquisition but as a holistic program investment. This perspective reflects their understanding that success in robotic surgery required more than the tools. It demanded building comprehensive programs capable of attracting top surgical talent and establishing sustainable market leadership.

Malcolm Gladwell's ten thousand hours to mastery principle underscores this urgency. With complex robotic procedures taking three to four hours each, achieving mastery (1,000–1,500 cases) required more than four thousand hours of focused practice. Strategic customers realized that early adoption provided a nearly insurmountable advantage in developing this expertise, reinforcing the importance of acting decisively.

Strategic customers are identified not only by their readiness to invest but also by their responsiveness to competitive challenges and their capacity to act definitively. Their decision-making frameworks balance the need for long-term program development with the immediate pressures of competitive dynamics. By doing so, they transform high-stakes investments into sustainable market leadership and redefine industry standards.

The Social Customer Perspective

While surgeons pioneered techniques and hospitals evaluated economics, social customers played a crucial role in helping robotic surgery deliver meaningful impact for patient communities. Organizations like the American Heart Association and American Cancer Society brought the patient perspective to the forefront, helping transform robotic surgery into a patient-centered advancement in care.

The American Cancer Society's efforts to support prostate cancer patients highlight the importance of ensuring individuals are well-informed about all available treatment options, both surgical and nonsurgical.[94] When early data suggested that robotic prostatectomy could reduce complications and speed recovery, the organization focused on providing balanced, accessible information rather than promoting any specific approach. They shared data showing how traditional open prostatectomies often involved longer hospital stays, greater pain, and higher risks of complications such as incontinence and erectile dysfunction, helping patients understand the potential benefits and risks of all procedures.

In addition to offering educational resources, the American Cancer Society established programs to help patients explore their options thoroughly. They created spaces where individuals could engage with others who had undergone different treatments, including robotic procedures, allowing for firsthand perspectives to complement clinical data. As one patient advocate explained to me, "Hearing directly from someone who's experienced it can make all the difference in helping patients feel confident in their choices." This commitment to education and connection enables patients to make decisions based on comprehensive, real-world insights tailored to their needs.

Similar patterns emerged in gynecologic oncology, where organizations representing cervical and endometrial cancer patients advocated for greater access to robotic surgery options. Their efforts highlighted disparities in access across different communities, with research and advocacy identifying significant gaps in availability. These findings led to the development of programs aimed at expanding access in underserved areas.[95]

As robotic surgery evolved, new organizations emerged specifically to support the robotic surgery community. Groups like the Clinical Robotic Surgery Association bridged the gap between innovation and patient benefit, creating forums where surgeons, patients, and advocacy groups could collaborate on improving outcomes.[96] These organizations helped establish patient-centered quality metrics that went beyond traditional surgical outcomes to include quality of life measures and patient satisfaction.

The impact of these social customers extended far beyond individual patient support. Their systematic collection of patient experiences and outcomes helped identify areas where additional support was needed. When they observed disparities in access to robotic surgery, they advocated for programs to expand availability in underserved communities. Their focus on inclusive access and patient education made it possible for the benefits of robotic surgery to reach diverse patient populations.

Through their unique combination of community advocacy and stakeholder engagement, social customers influenced the evolution of robotic surgery to prioritize not only technological advancement and economic viability, but also genuine patient benefit and community impact. Their influence helped robotic surgery mature from cutting-edge innovation to an adaptive model of care shaped by ongoing input from patients and communities.

APPENDIX B: LESSONS FROM ROBOTIC SURGERY (CFOSS® VALUE PROPOSITIONS)

Crafting Core Value Propositions Step by Step

The da Vinci Surgical System's CVPs offers an exemplary case of aligning with core customer needs through a structured, stepwise approach. For surgeons facing the constraints of traditional open surgery and laparoscopy, the system provided a transformative solution by enabling minimally invasive procedures for surgeries that had historically required open operations. Let's examine how this value proposition unfolded step by step.

Step 1: Understanding and Reflecting the Problem Connection

The da Vinci system began by addressing the deeply ingrained challenges surgeons faced in their daily practice. Open surgery was effective but came with significant drawbacks, including large incisions, prolonged recovery times, and increased patient discomfort. Traditional laparoscopy, although less invasive, introduced its own limitations, including restricted dexterity, suboptimal visualization, and difficulty performing complex procedures.

For core customers, surgeons dedicated to improving patient outcomes through minimally invasive surgery, these challenges were not abstract; they were daily obstacles that constrained their ability to provide optimal care. Demonstrating a profound understanding of these pain points, the da Vinci system validated the experiences of its core customers and established a meaningful connection with their professional realities.

Step 2: Highlighting Solution Impact

The da Vinci system didn't settle for incremental improvements; it redefined what was possible in surgery. The system enabled surgeons to perform minimally invasive procedures with unprecedented precision, dexterity, and visualization. These capabilities surpassed what traditional techniques could achieve.

For example, in a complex prostatectomy, the system allowed for precise movements in confined spaces, minimizing trauma to surrounding tissues. This advancement fundamentally transformed surgical capabilities, offering surgeons tools that allowed for outcomes previously unattainable without resorting to open surgery.

Step 3: Aligning with the Customer's Professional Mission

Beyond addressing technical challenges, the da Vinci system aligned seamlessly with surgeons' broader professional mission by improving patient outcomes and advancing the field of surgery. For these medical pioneers, the system supported their commitment to delivering the highest standard of care.

Minimally invasive surgery reduced recovery times, alleviated patient pain, and minimized complications, profoundly impacting patients' lives. At the same time, the system empowered surgeons to explore innovative techniques, pushing the boundaries of what was possible in their field. This alignment with both immediate patient care and the long-term evolution of surgical practice elevated the system from a technological advancement to a transformational force.

Crafting Financial Value Propositions Step by Step

To effectively communicate the FVP of the da Vinci Surgical System between 1999 and 2004, Intuitive Surgical employed a structured approach that addressed the priorities of financial customers.

Step 1: Economic Impact Assessment

Financial customers evaluating the da Vinci system required a clear understanding of its up-front costs and its potential to generate economic benefits. Hospitals faced significant capital expenses, including more than $1.5 million for the system itself, as well as ongoing training, maintenance, and per-procedure disposable costs. However, these expenses were offset by measurable savings and revenue opportunities.

The da Vinci system offered reduced hospital stays and minimized complications, leading to lower variable costs per patient. Improved recovery times enhanced bed turnover rates, enabling hospitals to serve more patients without increasing capacity. These efficiencies, combined with improved patient outcomes, underscored the system's ability to balance high initial investments with downstream cost savings and increased throughput.

Step 2: Financial Risk-Return Analysis

To bolster confidence in the da Vinci system's financial value, Intuitive Surgical framed its proposition with a risk-return analysis. Their perspective acknowledged both the rewards and the inherent risks of adoption.

Returns:

» Robotic-assisted procedures at times qualified for premium reimbursement categories, boosting revenue potential.
» Offering cutting-edge surgical capabilities helped hospitals attract more patients, particularly in competitive markets where innovation signaled quality.
» Early adoption established hospitals as leaders in minimally invasive surgery, securing market share gains that translated into sustained revenue growth.

Risks:

» The up-front cost posed a significant hurdle for hospitals with limited budgets.
» Justifying the investment required achieving sufficient procedure volumes, which was uncertain during early adoption stages.
» Onboarding surgeons created temporary productivity dips, potentially disrupting operations.
» Routine procedures without reimbursement premiums posed financial risks, requiring hospitals to prioritize high-margin surgeries strategically.

By transparently addressing these financial risks and pairing them with the potential returns, Intuitive Surgical empowered financial decision-makers to evaluate the da Vinci system as an investment within their fiscal constraints.

Step 3: Scalability Validation

To further reassure financial customers, Intuitive Surgical demonstrated the scalability of the da Vinci system and its ability to deliver sustained financial benefits over time. Hospitals were provided pathways to build robust revenue streams by increasing procedure volumes, expanding service lines, and optimizing operational efficiencies.

For instance, hospitals could begin by focusing on high-reimbursement specialties like urology and gynecology, gradually expanding the system's use to other disciplines such as general surgery and thoracic procedures. As adoption scaled, surgeon proficiency improved, disposable costs normalized, and operational workflows became more efficient. This scalability narrative underscored the system's ability to grow alongside hospital needs.

Crafting Operational Value Propositions Step by Step

Let's explore how the da Vinci system demonstrated its OVP through the three-step framework:

Step 1: Identifying Key Process Improvements

The da Vinci system addressed critical inefficiencies in hospital operations, particularly by reducing patient length of stay. Robotic-assisted surgeries minimized trauma and expedited recovery, enabling hospitals to discharge patients sooner. This improvement enhanced patient throughput and increased bed availability, allowing hospitals to treat more patients with existing resources.

Additionally, robotic surgery could reduce intraoperative bleeding compared to traditional open procedures. This innovation lowered the need for blood transfusions, decreasing direct costs and simplifying the logistics of blood delivery.

However, early adoption also revealed operational challenges, such as longer procedure times and extended setup processes. These hurdles underscored the importance of robust training programs and workflow optimization to unlock the full operational potential of robotic surgery.

Step 2: Measuring the Impact on Performance

Quantifiable metrics solidified the operational value of the da Vinci system over time. Reduced patient length of stay, faster bed turnover rates, and fewer intraoperative complications highlighted the system's tangible benefits. Hospitals treated more patients, optimized resource use, and reduced costs associated with prolonged recovery and postoperative care.

Although these gains were initially obscured by longer procedure times and setup challenges, they became clearer as hospitals refined workflows and expanded their robotic programs. Multirobot systems further amplified operational efficiency, enabling hospitals to address growing patient demands and maintain high standards of care.

Step 3: Focusing on Integration and Compatibility

Seamless integration into existing workflows was critical for operational customers to fully realize the benefits of robotic surgery. Early adopters faced challenges, such as adapting OR procedures and team dynamics. Compatibility with preexisting workflows was essential to minimize disruptions and maximize value.

Hospitals that successfully integrated the da Vinci system achieved impressive results. Streamlined workflows enabled quicker surgical turnovers, enhancing overall efficiency. Investments in training programs and scheduling adjustments helped mitigate initial challenges and facilitated smoother adoption.

As robotic programs expanded and hospitals incorporated multiple systems, integration became more effective. These advancements not only improved operational efficiency but also supported the broader adoption of robotic surgery across specialties, embedding the technology into standard practices.

This evolution underscores the dynamic nature of OVPs. Initial adoption may pose challenges, but the long-term gains in efficiency, resource optimization, and patient throughput highlight the lasting operational value of robotic surgery.

Crafting Strategic Value Propositions Step by Step

The da Vinci Surgical System became a strategic tool for hospitals to redefine their market positioning and establish leadership in minimally invasive surgery.

Let's examine the SVP of the da Vinci system through the three-step framework:

Step 1: Define the Strategic Advantage

Hospitals adopting the da Vinci system recognized the growing demand for minimally invasive surgery, driven by patients seeking faster recovery and less invasive procedures as well as by surgeons desiring advanced precision tools. Integrating the system provided a unique competitive edge, positioning hospitals as pioneers in cutting-edge surgical techniques. The system offered more than functional features; it provided strategic differentiation. Early adopters could brand themselves as centers of excellence for robotic surgery, attracting attention from patients, insurers, and referring physicians. For instance, the Vattikuti Urology Institute used the da Vinci system to draw renowned surgeon Dr. Mani Menon, whose expertise further elevated the institution's reputation. To many, robotic surgery symbolized innovation, signaling to stakeholders that these hospitals were investing in the future of patient care.

Step 2: Highlight Long-Term Growth Potential

The da Vinci system's value proposition extended beyond immediate benefits, offering hospitals a pathway to sustained growth. By adopting the system, institutions unlocked new revenue streams through robotic procedures that commanded higher reimbursement rates and attracted a wider patient base.

Hospitals that embraced the technology saw increased patient volumes, driven by a shift in expectations and preferences for robotic surgery. The ability to offer minimally invasive robotic procedures became a decisive factor for patients selecting healthcare providers, contributing to a steady flow of cases over the long term.

Additionally, the system enabled hospitals to expand their surgical offerings into complex procedures previously unsuitable for laparoscopy. This capability allowed institutions to diversify their specialties, reinforcing their status as leaders in advanced care and driving sustained competitive advantage.

Step 3: Align with Strategic Mission and Vision

For hospitals like Northside Hospital in Georgia, which is renowned for its commitment to women's health, the integration of the da Vinci system was particularly aligned with their strategic goals. Dr. Gerald Feuer, a leading surgeon at Northside, was instrumental in advocating for the system, seeing it as a transformative tool that would not only improve patient outcomes but also position the hospital as a pioneer in robotic minimally invasive surgery. Northside's decision to adopt robotic surgery reflected their commitment to providing the best possible care for women, especially in complex gynecological procedures, aligning with their mission of delivering excellence in women's health.

Moreover, this commitment went beyond clinical benefits. Early adoption of the da Vinci system showcased a forward-thinking approach, signaling a dedication to staying at the forefront of medical advancements. This alignment with Northside Hospital's strategic vision not only attracted top surgical talent but also inspired confidence among patients and stakeholders. By prominently featuring robotic surgery in marketing and outreach efforts, Northside further established itself as a leader in healthcare innovation. Patients saw the hospital as a place where cutting-edge technology was used to improve their health, and surgeons viewed it as an ideal environment for practicing advanced surgical techniques.

Crafting Social Value Propositions Step by Step

Robotic surgery during the early 2000s offers a compelling example of how SoVPs can transcend traditional healthcare innovation to create broader societal benefits.

Let's examine its SoVP through the lens of the three-step framework:

Step 1: Identify the Broader Societal Impact

The da Vinci system offered transformative benefits by addressing health disparities and providing access to advanced medical care. For example, prostate cancer, which disproportionately affects Black men, represented a critical area where robotic-assisted prostatectomies could make a meaningful impact.[97] As robotic surgery became the leading treatment option for prostatectomies, its ability to minimize surgical trauma, reduce complications, and expedite recovery times held significant potential for improving outcomes for this high-risk group.

Similarly, robotic cardiac surgery provided a life-saving option for high-risk patients by reducing the morbidity and mortality associated with traditional open-heart surgeries.[98] The societal impact of these improvements extended beyond individual patients, benefiting entire communities and the healthcare systems that served them.

Step 2: Demonstrate Authentic Commitment to Purpose

Robotic surgery demonstrated a genuine commitment to inclusivity and patient-centered care. A striking example of this was its alignment with the needs of Jehovah's Witnesses, who may not accept blood transfusions because of their religious beliefs.[99] Traditional surgeries posed significant risks of blood loss, but the precision and minimally invasive nature of robotic techniques provided a crucial alternative. Minimizing transfusion needs, the da Vinci system enabled life-saving care and honored patients' deeply held convictions.

Step 3: Align with Customer Values and Movements

Again, by addressing prostate cancer disparities among Black men, robotic surgery aligned with the mission of organizations such as the American Cancer Society, which advocates for equitable access to advanced treatment options.

Hospitals that adopted the da Vinci system often collaborated with advocacy groups to raise awareness about minimally invasive surgical options. These partnerships amplified the social impact of robotic surgery by keeping patients and families informed about advanced care solutions. Such collaborations strengthened trust between medical institutions and the communities they served, while simultaneously enhancing healthcare accessibility.

APPENDIX C: CFOSS® ARCHETYPE VALUE MATRIX

This matrix offers a practical lens for applying the CFOSS framework by mapping out how different customer archetypes experience your value propositions. For each of the five CFOSS pillars you'll find a breakdown of customer scenarios, behaviors, emotional responses, and common concerns. Use this tool to surface alignment gaps, craft targeted messaging, and develop offerings that connect with your market's distinct priorities.

CORE VALUE PROPOSITION

CORE CUSTOMER	FINANCIAL CUSTOMER	OPERATIONAL CUSTOMER	STRATEGIC CUSTOMER	SOCIAL CUSTOMER
Scenario: Finds the product intuitive, reliable, and simple to use **Behavior:** Quickly integrates it into their routine, sharing positive feedback with others seeking similar solutions **Feelings:** Empowered, satisfied, and relieved to have a seamless solution **Opportunity:** Emphasize long-term durability and ease of use in marketing materials	**Scenario:** Perceives the product as potentially costly without clear savings **Behavior:** Compares alternatives and scrutinizes pricing for value **Feelings:** Frustrated, undervalued, wary of hidden costs **Concerns:** Pricing model doesn't reflect their need for cost-effectiveness	**Scenario:** Intrigued but cautious about how well the product fits into their workflow **Behavior:** Attempts to adapt it but may experience friction without customization **Feelings:** Curious but disappointed if it disrupts their processes **Concerns:** Seeks seamless integration and minimal disruption	**Scenario:** Stifles a yawn, feeling underwhelmed by the lack of advantage **Behavior:** Quickly loses interest, seeking out competitors who offer cutting-edge solutions **Feelings:** Uninspired, unconvinced of the product's competitive edge **Concerns:** Product lacks features compared to competitors; doesn't align with their future ambitions	**Scenario:** Evaluates the product's alignment with their values **Behavior:** Seeks a balance between practical features and ethical practices **Feelings:** Cautious but optimistic when value alignment is present **Concerns:** Needs transparency and authentic claims about social responsibility

FINANCIAL VALUE PROPOSITION

CORE CUSTOMER	FINANCIAL CUSTOMER	OPERATIONAL CUSTOMER	STRATEGIC CUSTOMER	SOCIAL CUSTOMER
Scenario: Hesitates, unsure if cost savings compromise functionality	**Scenario:** Quickly recognizes the potential for cost savings and ROI	**Scenario:** Questions the connection between financial savings and operational gains	**Scenario:** Sees short-term cost savings as irrelevant to their long-term vision	**Scenario:** Analyzes cost savings for ethical compromises
Behavior: Seeks proof that the product addresses core needs	**Behavior:** Eagerly calculates benefits, shares insights with peers, and champions the value	**Behavior:** Demands evidence of how the product reduces operational costs	**Behavior:** Refocuses conversations on sustainable competitive advantages	**Behavior:** Investigates labor practices and sourcing
Feelings: Cautious, needing reassurance before committing	**Feelings:** Confident, empowered by their financially sound decision	**Feelings:** Skeptical without data or detailed case studies.	**Feelings:** Disengaged, unimpressed by narrow cost-focused pitches	**Feelings:** Wary of potential conflicts with values
Concerns: Requires evidence of value without sacrificing effectiveness	**Opportunity:** Highlight ROI through compelling data and competitive pricing	**Concerns:** Worries about missing key operational features	**Concerns:** Needs long-term profitability assurances	**Concerns:** Needs evidence that monetary savings don't come at an ethical cost

OPERATIONAL VALUE PROPOSITION

CORE CUSTOMER	FINANCIAL CUSTOMER	OPERATIONAL CUSTOMER	STRATEGIC CUSTOMER	SOCIAL CUSTOMER
Scenario: Needs the product to reliably address specific pain points **Behavior**: Quickly redirects focus to whether it solves their immediate problem **Feelings**: Frustrated or disconnected, feels like the solution is designed for the system, not them **Concerns**: Does this actually solve the problem I came here to fix?	**Scenario**: Evaluates potential cost savings against the need for quality and durability **Behavior**: Analyzes detailed data and comparisons to validate financial benefits **Feelings**: Analytical, needing clear evidence of ROI **Concerns**: Worries that operational gains may not fully justify costs without tangible financial returns	**Scenario**: Thrilled to see seamless integration and improved productivity **Behavior**: Eagerly adopts the product and shares positive feedback **Feelings**: Empowered, satisfied with enhanced workflows **Opportunity**: Provide ongoing support for sustained success	**Scenario**: Questions how operational efficiency supports broader goals **Behavior**: Requests a road map linking efficiency to innovation and growth **Feelings**: Engaged but needs strategic justification **Concerns**: Wants assurances of scalability and strategic fit	**Scenario**: Evaluates whether operational efficiency aligns with their ethical and sustainability values **Behavior**: Evaluates how operational efficiency supports social impact goals, focusing on community benefits **Feelings**: Hopeful but cautious about potential conflicts between values and efficiency **Concerns**: Demands that operational gains are achieved without compromising ethical standards or sustainability efforts

STRATEGIC VALUE PROPOSITION

CORE CUSTOMER	FINANCIAL CUSTOMER	OPERATIONAL CUSTOMER	STRATEGIC CUSTOMER	SOCIAL CUSTOMER
Scenario: Focused on practical solutions, disengaged by abstract strategy **Behavior**: Prioritizes immediate benefits over long-term visions **Feelings**: Confused, uninterested in theoretical discussions **Concerns**: Seeks tangible, actionable solutions to current challenges	**Scenario**: Needs financial justification for long-term strategy alignment **Behavior**: Demands clear ROI projections **Feelings**: Skeptical of abstract, unproven claims **Concerns**: Prioritizes near-term profitability	**Scenario**: Resists strategic changes that disrupt workflows **Behavior**: Focuses on maintaining current operational efficiency **Feelings**: Overwhelmed, cautious about change **Concerns**: Needs assurances of minimal disruption	**Scenario**: Eagerly explores opportunities for market leadership **Behavior**: Partners with aligned innovations for competitive advantage **Feelings**: Inspired, energized by shared vision **Opportunity**: Highlight partnerships and long-term potential	**Scenario**: Evaluates how market leadership benefits the community **Behavior**: Advocates for solutions that prioritize societal impact and inclusivity **Feelings**: Hopeful but cautious about alignment with community values **Concerns**: Seeks assurances that leadership fosters positive societal outcomes

APPENDIX C: CFOSS® ARCHETYPE VALUE MATRIX | 193

SOCIAL VALUE PROPOSITION

CORE CUSTOMER	FINANCIAL CUSTOMER	OPERATIONAL CUSTOMER	STRATEGIC CUSTOMER	SOCIAL CUSTOMER
Scenario: Values practicality over social messaging	**Scenario**: Skeptical of social benefits without financial proof	**Scenario**: Balances efficiency with ethical considerations	**Scenario**: Values social impact for brand and competitive positioning	**Scenario**: Expects innovations to reflect genuine community benefit.
Behavior: Evaluates the product for functionality	**Behavior**: Investigates ROI on sustainability initiatives	**Behavior**: Avoids complexity caused by social initiatives	**Behavior**: Engages with companies showing authentic social leadership	**Behavior**: Actively supports companies whose actions consistently align with stated values
Feelings: Neutral if impact feels disconnected	**Feelings**: Wary of perceived inefficiencies	**Feelings**: Respectful but focused on operations	**Feelings**: Optimistic but cautious	**Feelings**: Inspired and loyal when impact is authentic and sustained
Concerns: Social focus must complement usability	**Concerns**: Needs financial alignment with ethical practices	**Concerns**: Social goals should not hinder processes	**Concerns**: Seeks consistency in values and actions	**Opportunity**: Demonstrate authenticity through consistent, community-rooted actions

APPENDIX D: LESSONS FROM ROBOTIC SURGERY (CFOSS® MISMATCHES)

The da Vinci Surgical System, introduced by Intuitive Surgical, promised to revolutionize minimally invasive surgery. However, its early adoption was fraught with challenges that stemmed from mismatches between its value propositions and the needs of various customer archetypes. The system showed significant potential in improving patient outcomes, but adoption was slow as hospitals struggled to align the technology with their operational, financial, strategic, and social priorities. This case study explores the key CFOSS value proposition mismatches that occurred during robotic surgery's early adoption and examines how these misalignments impacted the adoption process.

CFOSS Mismatches

Core Customer Misalignment

The da Vinci system was initially positioned as a solution to minimally invasive cardiothoracic fundamental surgical problems, such as reducing patient recovery times and improving precision. However, the system failed to meet the immediate and practical needs of core customers during its early stages. The system required a steep learning curve, and many surgeons found its complexity to be a barrier to quick adoption. Surgeons focused on the immediate benefits of the technology, such as its ability to reduce scarring and pain, did not initially see the system as solving their daily surgical challenges, particularly in terms of ease of use and workflow integration. As a result, many cardiothoracic surgeons were hesitant to adopt the system, leading to misalignment between the product's value proposition and their problem-solving needs.

Financial Customer Misalignment

Financial customers found it difficult to justify the high up-front costs of the da Vinci system. With prices exceeding $1 million per unit, financial decision-makers struggled to see the immediate ROI, especially in light of limited reimbursement for robotic procedures. The system promised to reduce hospital stays and improve surgical outcomes, but the financial benefits remained unclear at the outset. CFOs raised concerns about the ongoing service contracts, disposable instruments, and training costs, which made the economic proposition of the system less compelling. In some cases, hospitals were unable to proceed with adoption, as financial decision-makers prioritized cost-effectiveness over the long-term benefits, contributing to a significant misalignment with the value propositions.

Operational Customer Misalignment

Operational customers, including hospital administrators and operating room managers, faced challenges in integrating the da Vinci system into existing workflows. In some cases, the robotic system required significant modifications to operating room layouts, added complexity to surgical procedures, and introduced new maintenance and staff training requirements. Administrators were concerned about the disruption to existing operations and the added burden on hospital staff to adapt to the new technology. The OVP of the da Vinci system was not immediately clear, while it promised to improve outcomes, it was difficult to quantify how it would directly enhance operational efficiency in the short term. The failure to clearly demonstrate how the system would integrate with existing workflows led to operational pushback, making it harder to secure hospital buy-in.

Strategic Customer Misalignment

At the strategic level, hospital executives struggled to see how the da Vinci system aligned with their long-term growth objectives. Despite its innovation, some hospital leaders did not view the technology as essential for gaining a competitive advantage or establishing market leadership. For many hospitals, the focus was on immediate financial stability and operational efficiency, not necessarily longterm differentiation or leadership in robotic surgery. Hospital executives questioned whether investing in such expensive technology would provide them with a significant competitive edge or market positioning in an increasingly crowded healthcare environment.

Social Customer Misalignment

Social customers, including patient advocacy groups and the general public, were concerned about the social implications of adopting the da Vinci system. The system promised improved patient outcomes, such as shorter recovery times and fewer complications, but also posed a significant financial burden that risked exacerbating healthcare inequality. Patient groups questioned whether the high cost of robotic surgery would limit its accessibility to underserved populations, creating a disparity in access to cutting-edge medical technology. Additionally, the system's environmental impact, such as the disposable instruments it required, raised concerns about its sustainability.

Exploring the Consequences of Mismatches

The misalignments in the CFOSS value propositions had several significant consequences for the early adoption of the da Vinci Surgical System:

» **Prolonged Sales Cycles:** The hesitations from financial and operational customers led to prolonged sales cycles, as hospitals struggled to see the immediate value in the system.

» **Increased Cost of Sales:** The lack of alignment between the system's value propositions and the needs of various customer archetypes meant that Intuitive Surgical had to invest significantly in educating customers, particularly financial and operational decision-makers. This increased the cost of sales, as the company had to show the system's value repeatedly through case studies and demonstrations.

» **Reduced Conversion Rates:** Despite strong initial interest, many hospitals ultimately decided not to purchase the system because of the misalignment between their needs and the value proposition offered. The reduced conversion rate meant that the company missed out on potential sales and had to focus more resources on customer education and engagement.

» **High Customer Turnover:** Some early customers who adopted the system quickly became disillusioned because of the challenges they faced during integration and the higher-than-expected ongoing costs. This led to higher customer turnover as hospitals abandoned the technology or chose not to invest in additional systems.

» **Stifled Revenue Growth:** The slow adoption of the system limited Intuitive Surgical's ability to scale quickly. As a result, revenue growth was stifled in the early years, and the company faced challenges in reaching critical mass in its customer base.

Addressing Mismatches: Solutions and Adjustments

In response to the challenges faced during the early adoption of the da Vinci Surgical System, Intuitive Surgical implemented several adjustments to align the technology with customer needs, improving adoption across the CFOSS archetypes.

For core customers, Intuitive Surgical simplified the user interface and worked to make the system more intuitive, addressing concerns about the complexity of the technology. They focused on user-friendliness, allowing surgeons to quickly integrate the system into their daily routines. To further align with core customer needs, Intuitive Surgical also established regular feedback loops with surgeons. This enabled the company to make iterative refinements based on real-world experience, resulting in a system that more effectively addressed surgeons' needs.

For financial customers, Intuitive Surgical revised its financial model to demonstrate the long-term ROI and cost-effectiveness of the da Vinci system. They created detailed case studies showing the financial impact of the system, which highlighted not only the potential for improved patient outcomes but also the cost savings in the long run. Additionally, they introduced more flexible payment options, including leasing and financing programs, making the system more accessible to hospitals facing budget constraints.

Intuitive Surgical adapted the da Vinci system to fit more easily into hospital workflows, responding to operational customer priorities. They introduced structured integration plans, providing hospitals with clear road maps to help adapt the system to their unique operational needs. In support of operational efficiency, dedicated teams were put in place to provide training, integration guidance, and technical support, helping hospitals navigate the transition with minimal disruption.

For strategic customers, Intuitive Surgical repositioned the da Vinci system as a key component of a hospital's long-term growth strategy. They emphasized the system's potential to help hospitals stay competitive by attracting top surgical talent and providing cutting-edge technology. Intuitive Surgical highlighted how robotic surgery could serve as a differentiator in a crowded market, making it an essential tool for hospitals striving for leadership in the healthcare space.

To better align with social customers, Intuitive Surgical engaged more closely with patient advocacy groups. They demonstrated the system's potential to improve patient community outcomes. These efforts helped to build trust and broaden the adoption of the system across different customer segments.

Key Takeaways for Innovators

The case study of the early adoption of the da Vinci Surgical System offers critical lessons for innovators seeking to navigate the complexities of aligning value propositions with customer needs. One of the most significant takeaways is that alignment across all CFOSS dimensions are absolutely crucial. A mismatch in even one of these areas can derail adoption and prevent or slow down an innovation from achieving market success. The challenges faced by Intuitive Surgical in the early stages of the da Vinci's adoption highlight how vital it is for innovators to address the unique needs and expectations of each customer archetype.

Another key lesson is the importance of continuous feedback and adaptation. Intuitive Surgical's ability to evolve the da Vinci Surgical System in response to feedback from surgeons, hospital administrators, and financial decision-makers ultimately helped the system gain traction in the market. To remain relevant, innovators must gather feedback from all customer archetypes and continuously refine their value propositions in response to evolving priorities and market dynamics.

Proactive alignment strategies also emerged as crucial in the case of the da Vinci system. By anticipating and addressing potential misalignments early on, Intuitive Surgical minimized friction points in the sales process and built stronger relationships with its customer base. Innovators can learn from this proactive approach, aligning value propositions across all CFOSS dimensions from the outset. This prevents the pitfalls of misalignment and fosters smoother adoption.

APPENDIX D: LESSONS FROM ROBOTIC SURGERY (CFOSS® MISMATCHES)

ENDNOTES

i. 2013 Annual Report (Intuitive Surgical).

ii. Moore, *Crossing the Chasm*.

iii. The technology adoption life cycle (TALC) was popularized by Geoffrey A. Moore in his influential book *Crossing the Chasm: Marketing and Selling High-Tech Products to Mainstream Customers* (HarperBusiness, 1991). Moore expanded on the original concept, introducing the idea of a chasm between early adopters and the early majority, which is particularly relevant for disruptive innovations. Image redesigned by Jenée Baker, 2025

iv. *Annual Report* (Computer Motion, 2002).

v. *2009 Annual Report* (Intuitive Surgical).

vi. Tony Scherba, "Remembering Microsoft's Zune: 4 Product-Planning Lessons," *Entrepreneur*, accessed December 24, 2024, https://www.entrepreneur.com/business-news/remembering-microsofts-zune-4-product-planning-lessons/286490.

vii. Walter Isaacson, *Steve Jobs* (Simon & Schuster, 2011), 391–395.

viii. Adityabikram Singh et al, "Comparison of Robotic-Assisted and Laparoscopic Cholecystectomy: Outcomes and Costs," *Surgery* 173, no. 6 (2023): 1323–1328, https://www.surgjournal.com/article/S0039-6060(23)00043-0/abstract.

ix. "Our Customer Promise: Uplift the Everyday," Starbucks, last modified 2024, https://about.starbucks.com/our-customer-promise-uplift-the-everyday/#thirdplace.

x. "Amazon Introduces Same-Day Delivery," Amazon, May 1, 2014, https://press.aboutamazon.com/news-releases/news-release-details/amazon-introduces-same-day-delivery.

xi. Joseph A. Michelli, *The Starbucks Experience: 5 Principles for Turning Ordinary Into Extraordinary* (McGraw-Hill, 2006), 51–55.

xii. Adam Reeves, "Why Facebook's Acquisition of Instagram Was a Smart Move," *The Motley Fool*, last modified November 26, 2013, https://www.fool.com/investing/general/2013/11/26/why-facebooks-acquisition-of-instagram-was-a-smart.aspx.

xiii. Brad Stone, *The Everything Store: Jeff Bezos and the Age of Amazon* (Little, Brown and Company, 2013).

xiv. "Buy a Pair, Give a Pair," Warby Parker, accessed December 24, 2024. https://www.warbyparker.com/buy-a-pair-give-a-pair.

xv. Dana Scarton, "The Importance of the Pinkie, Experienced Firsthand," *New York Times*, December 16, 2008, https://www.nytimes.com/2008/12/18/health/18iht-snpinkie.1.18718834.html.

xvi. "$20M Community-Driven Research Funding Aims to Reduce Inequities, Improve Health Outcomes," American Heart Association, last modified June 9, 2022, https://newsroom.heart.org/news/20m-community-driven-research-funding-aims-to-reduce-inequities-improve-health-outcomes.

xvii. "C.A.F.E. Practices: Starbucks Approach to Ethically Sourcing Coffee," Starbucks, accessed December 24, 2024, https://www.starbucks.com/responsibility/sourcing/coffee/.

xviii. E.M. Rogers, *Diffusion of Innovations*, 5th ed. (Free Press, 2003).

xix. Moore, *Crossing the Chasm*.

xx. "Healthcare-associated infections," CDC, updated June 21, 2021, https://www.cdc.gov/policy/polaris/healthtopics/hai/index.html (site discontinued).

xxi. Dan Roam, *The Back of the Napkin: Solving Problems and Selling Ideas with Pictures* (Portfolio, 2008).

xxii. Dr. Obi Ugwonali and Dana Weeks, presentation to Dr. Baker's class, Georgia State University, November 4, 2024.

xxiii. "Missed Appointments Cost the U.S. Healthcare System $150B Each Year," Healthcare Innovation, last modified May 1, 2018, https://www.hcinnovationgroup.com/clinical-it/article/13008175/missed-appointments-cost-the-us-healthcare-system-150b-each-year.

xxiv. "About Us," Metric Mate, accessed September 30, 2024, https://www.themetricmate.com/aboutus.

xxv. "Gerald Feuer," Atlanta Gynecologic Oncology, accessed December 24, 2024, https://atlantagynonc.com/providers/gerald-feuer.

xxvi. "About RICE," Russell Innovation Center for Entrepreneurs, accessed September 30, 2024, https://russellcenter.org/about-us/.

xxvii. "The RICE Report, Volume 1," Russell Center, revised February 1, 2025, https://russellcenter.org/wp-content/uploads/2025/02/The-RICE-Report_Digital-Download-rev-020125.pdf.

xxviii. "About Goodie Nation," Goodie Nation, accessed December 24, 2024, https://goodienation.org/about/.

xxix. "About ATDC," ATDC, accessed December 24, 2024, https://atdc.org/about-overview/.

xxx. The National Veteran-Owned Business Association (NaVOBA), accessed December 24, 2024, https://navoba.org/.

xxxi. "Thrive Farmers Coffee," Chick-fil-A, accessed September 30, 2024, https://www.chick-fil-a.com/stories/inside-chick-fil-a/thrive-farmers-coffee.

xxxii. Jay B. Barney, "Firm Resources and Sustained Competitive Advantage," *Journal of Management* 17, no. 1 (1991): 99–120, https://doi.org/10.1177/014920639101700108.

xxxiii. Richard Normann and Rafael Ramirez, "Designing Interactive Strategy," *Harvard Business Review* HBR 71.4 (July 1993), 65–77, retrieved from https://hbr.org/1993/07/designing-interactive-strategy.

xxxiv. Christian Grönroos, "Service Logic Revisited: Who Creates Value? And Who Co-creates?," *European Business Review* 20, no. 4 (2008): 298–314, https://doi.org/10.1108/09555340810886585; Stanley F. Slater, "Developing a Customer Value-Based Theory of the Firm," *Journal of the Academy of Marketing Science* 25, no. 2 (1997): 162–167, https://doi.org/10.1007/BF02894352

xxxv. Michael E. Porter, *Competitive Advantage: Creating and Sustaining Superior Performance* (Free Press, 1985); Ajay Menon, Christian Homburg, Nikolas Beutin, and Mark Colgate, "Product and Company Identification: A Conceptual Framework of Drivers and Outcomes," *Industrial Marketing Management* 34, no. 1 (2005): 4-17, https://doi.org/10.1016/j.indmarman.2004.07.001.

xxxvi. Clayton M. Christensen and Michael E. Raynor, *The Innovator's Solution: Creating and Sustaining Successful Growth* (Harvard Business School Press, 2003).

xxxvii. Eric Ries, *The Lean Startup: How Today's Entrepreneurs Use Continuous Innovation to Create Radically Successful Businesses* (Crown Business, 2011).

xxxviii. Alexander Osterwalder and Yves Pigneur, *Business Model Generation: A Handbook for Visionaries, Game Changers, and Challengers* (John Wiley & Sons, 2010).

xxxix. G. Spinoglio et al, "Single-Site Robotic Cholecystectomy (SSRC) versus Single-Incision Laparoscopic Cholecystectomy (SILC): Comparison of Learning Curves. First European Experience," *Surgical Endoscopy*, 26 no. 6 (2012), 1648–1655.

xl. Brad Stone, *Amazon Unbound: Jeff Bezos and the Invention of a Global Empire* (Simon & Schuster, 2021), 15–20.

xli. Stone, *Amazon Unbound*, 15–20.

xlii. "Amazon Prime Rewards Visa Signature Card," Amazon, accessed October 5, 2024, https://www.amazon.com/Amazon-Prime-Rewards-Visa-Signature-Card/dp/B07CBJQS16

xliii. "Chick-fil-A One® Rewards Program Terms and Conditions," Chick-fil-A, accessed October 5, 2024, https://www.chick-fil-a.com/legal/one-program-terms

xliv. Garth H. Ballantyne, "Robotic Surgery, Telerobotic Surgery, Telepresence, and Telementoring," *Surgical Endoscopy* 16, no. 10 (2002): 1389–1402, https://doi.org/10.1007/s00464-001-8283-7

xlv. "FedEx Earns Historic 30-Year ISO 9001 Certification," FedEx, accessed December 24, 2024, https://newsroom.fedex.com/newsroom/global-english/fedex-earns-historic-30-year-iso-9001-certification.

xlvi. "Starbucks Mobile Order & Pay Now Available to Customers Nationwide," Starbucks, press release, September 22, 2015, https://stories.starbucks.com/press/2015/starbucks-mobile-order-pay-now-available-to-customers-nationwide/.

xlvii. *2004 Annual Report* (Intuitive Surgical, March 11, 2005), https://isrg.gcs-web.com/static-files/b1c2d9f6-4b0b-4042-a4b1-1f4b8b3c3f8a

xlviii. Ryan Johnson, Bugle founder, presentation to Dr. Baker's class, Georgia State University, September 23, 2024.

xlix. "Firehouse Subs Partners with Coca-Cola Freestyle," Coca-Cola Company, Coca-Cola Journey, May 1, 2011, https://www.coca-colacompany.com/news/firehouse-subs-partners-with-coca-cola-freestyle

l. "Firehouse Subs Celebrates 25th Anniversary with Nationwide Launch of Coca-Cola Freestyle 9100," PR Newswire, August 15, 2019, https://www.prnewswire.com/news-releases/firehouse-subs-celebrates-25th-anniversary-with-nationwide-launch-of-coca-cola-freestyle-9100-300902030.html

li. S. Truett Cathy, *Eat Mor Chikin: Inspire More People* (Looking Glass Books, 2002), 100–102.

lii. "The QSR 50," *QSR Magazine*, August 2022, https://www.qsrmagazine.com/content/qsr50-2022-top-50-chart

liii. "Fiscal 2022 Annual Report" (Starbucks Corporation, November 18, 2022), https://s22.q4cdn.com/869488222/files/doc_financials/2022/ar/Starbucks-Corporation-FY22-Annual-Report.pdf.

liv. *2004 Annual Report* (Intuitive Surgical).

lv. Vipul R. Patel, "The Early Experience with Robot-Assisted Radical Prostatectomy," in *Robotic Urologic Surgery*, ed. Vipul R. Patel (Springer-Verlag, 2007), 3–9, https://doi.org/10.1007/978-1-84628-545-5_1.

lvi. R. Edward Freeman, "Stakeholder Capitalism and Creating Value for All Stakeholders," presentation at J. Mack Robinson College of Business, Georgia State University, Atlanta, Georgia, October 12, 2022, https://robinson.gsu.edu/event/stakeholder-capitalism-and-creating-value-for-all-stakeholders/

lvii. "Report on US Sustainable and Impact Investing Trends 2020," US SIF Foundation, accessed September 30, 2024, https://www.ussif.org/trends.

lviii. "Environmental + Social Initiatives," Patagonia, accessed October 7, 2024, https://www.patagonia.com/environmental-social-initiatives.html.

lix. "Introducing Justice ReMix'd," Ben & Jerry's, last modified September 2019, https://www.benjerry.com/whats-new/2019/09/introducing-justice-remixd.

lx. "Impact," TOMS, accessed December 24, 2024, https://www.toms.com/us/impact.html.

lxi. "Pokket™: Empowering Justice-Involved Individuals," Acivilate, Inc., accessed September 30, 2024, https://www.acivilate.com/pokket

lxii. "Water, Sanitation and Hygiene (WASH)," UNICEF, accessed October 7, 2024, https://www.unicef.org/wash.

lxiii. "Southwest's Fleet Initiatives Are Helping Preserve Its Low-Cost Advantage," *Forbes*, last modified February 28, 2014, https://www.forbes.com/sites/greatspeculations/2014/02/28/southwests-fleet-initiatives-are-helping-preserve-its-low-cost-advantage/.

lxiv. David Koenig, "Southwest Airlines to Introduce Assigned Seating and Premium Perks," AP News, last modified December 6, 2024, https://apnews.com/article/southwest-changes-seating-boarding-hedge-fund-ba6a97380df6201e9a35335d3202fc8a.

lxv. Brad Templeton, "Uber's Lawlessness Began with Good Intentions—Could It Have Been Saved from Going Wrong?" *Forbes*, last modified July 11, 2022, https://www.forbes.com/sites/bradtempleton/2022/07/11/ubers-lawlessness-began-with-good-intentions-could-it-have-been-saved-from-going-wrong/.

lxvi. Real Engineering. 2020. *Why Was Normandy Selected For D-Day?* Youtube, March 28. https://www.youtube.com/watch?v=sYX-YG_F1EK0.

lxvii. Real Engineering. 2020. *Why Was Normandy Selected For D-Day?* Youtube, March 28. https://www.youtube.com/watch?v=sYX-YG_F1EK0.

lxviii. Becker, Sam. 2014. *What are the Odds that Your Startup Will Receive Funding From an Angel Investor?* Accessed August 18, 2021. https://www.alleywatch.com/2014/01/what-are-the-odds-that-your-startup-will-receive-funding-from-an-angel-investor.

lxix. Rao, Dileep. 2013. *Why 99.95% Of Entrepreneurs Should Stop Wasting Time Seeking Venture Capital.* July 22. Accessed August 18, 2021. https://www.forbes.com/sites/dileeprao/2013/07/22/why-99-95-of-entrepreneurs-should-stop-wasting-time-seeking-venture-capital/.

lxx. Liu, Sifan, and Joseph Parilla. 2019. *Is America's Seed Fund investing in women- and minority-owned businesses?* June 4. Accessed August 18, 2021. https://www.brookings.edu/blog/the-avenue/2019/06/04/is-americas-seed-fund-investing-in-women-and-minority-owned-businesses/.

lxxi. Pardes, Arielle. 2020. *Yet Another Year of Venture Capital Being Really White.* December 29. Accessed August 18, 2021. https://www.wired.com/story/venture-capital-2020-still-really-white/.

lxxii. Aleman, Zimena. 2020. *Startup fundraising is the most tangible gender gap. How can we overcome it?* November 10. Accessed August 18, 2021. https://social.techcrunch.com/2020/11/09/startup-fundraising-is-the-most-tangible-gender-gap-how-can-we-overcome-it/.

lxxiii. Kerr-Dineen, Luke. 2016. *Here are your odds of becoming a professional athlete (they're not good).* July 27. Accessed August 18, 2021. https://ftw.usatoday.com/2016/07/here-are-your-odds-of-becoming-a-professional-athlete-theyre-not-good.

lxxiv. Inc.Staff. 2012. *How Spanx Got Started.* January 12. Accessed August 18, 2021. https://www.inc.com/sara-blakely/how-sara-blakley-started-spanx.html

lxxv. Briody, Blaire. 2018. *Sara Blakely: Start Small, Think Big, Scale Fast.* June 21. Accessed August 18, 2021. https://www.gsb.stanford.edu/insights/sara-blakely-start-small-think-big-scale-fast.

lxxvi. 1995. *Apollo 13.* Directed by Howard Ron. Performed by Tom Hanks.

lxxvii. Blakely, Sara. 2021. *Sara Blakely Teaches Self-Made Entrepreneurship.* Accessed August 18, 2021. https://www.masterclass.com/classes/sara-blakely-teaches-self-made-entrepreneurship.

lxxviii. Briody, Blaire. 2018. *Sara Blakely: Start Small, Think Big, Scale Fast.* June 21. Accessed August 18, 2021. https://www.gsb.stanford.edu/

insights/sara-blakely-start-small-think-big-scale-fast.

lxxix. Intuitive Surgical. 2004 *Annual Report*. Sunnyvale, CA: Intuitive Surgical.

lxxx. 2013. *The Story of SPANX: Company Timeline*. Accessed August 18, 2021. http://press.spanx.com/_ir/117/20131/Vertical%20Timeline_16x10_2.6.pdf.

lxxxi. W.J. Chitwood, A.P. Kypson, and L.W. Nifong, "Robotic Mitral Valve Surgery: A Technologic and Economic Revolution for Heart Centers," The American Heart Hospital Journal, 1 no. 1 (2003): 30–39.

lxxxii. M. Menon, A. Tewari, B. Baize, B. Guillonneau, and G. Vallancien, "Prospective Comparison of Radical Retropubic Prostatectomy and Robot-Assisted Anatomic Prostatectomy: The Vattikuti Urology Institute Experience," Urology 60, no. 5 (2002): 864–868, https://doi.org/10.1016/S0090-4295(02)01881-2

lxxxiii. 2004 Annual Report (Intuitive Surgical).

lxxxiv. P. Sooriakumaran et al, "Learning Curve for Robotic Assisted Laparoscopic Prostatectomy: A Multi-institutional Study of 3794 Patients," Minerva urologica e nefrologica (The Italian Journal of Urology and Nephrology), 63 no. 3 (2011): 191–198.

lxxxv. "History of the Vattikuti Urology Institute," Henry Ford Health System, 2014, retrieved From http://www.henryford.com/body.cfm?id=38735

lxxxvi. "Orlando's Bid to Become a Medical Destination Receives Major Boost with Arrival of Internationally Recognized Surgeon, Robotic Institute," Florida Hospital Media Relations, January 18, 2008, retrieved from http://www.floridahospitalnews.com/florida-hospital-welcomes-dr-patel-lead-robotics-institute.

lxxxvii. "AAGL Position Statement: Robotic-Assisted Laparoscopic Surgery in Benign Gynecology," J Minimally Invasive Gynecol, 20 no. 1 (2013): 2–9, retrieved from Elsevier

lxxxviii. "Health Care 2017: Envisioning Our Future," Catholic Health East Horizons, 2006, retrieved from http://www.che.org/publications/pdf/H2006S.pdf

lxxxix. "Orlando's Bid to Become a Medical Destination," Florida Hospital Media Relations.

xc. Berkley Baker, "The Role of Industry Structure on Customer Value in Robotic Surgery" (DBA diss., Georgia State University, 2015).

xci.	G.I. Barbash and S.A. Glied, "New Technology and Health Care Costs—The Case of Robot-Assisted Surgery," New England Journal of Medicine, 363 no. 8 (2010): 701–704.
xcii.	Sooriakumaran, "Learning Curve for Robotic Assisted Laparoscopic Prostatectomy."
xciii.	P. Imbesi, "Chicago Medical Center Attracts Robotic Expert," IndUS Business Journal, December 15, 2007, retrieved from http://www.indusbusinessjournal.com/ME2/Sites/dirmod.asp?sid=&nm=&type=Publishing&mod=Publications%3A%3AArticle&mid=-8F3A7027421841978F18BE895F87F791&tier=4&id=40D37DD296504FF0ADB851F002D0B039&SiteID=Main%20Si_e (site discontinued).
xciv.	"Surgery for Prostate Cancer," American Cancer Society, accessed December 24, 2024, https://www.cancer.org/cancer/types/prostate-cancer/treating/surgery.html.
xcv.	Koji Matsuo, Susan L. Hendrix, Keisuke Kawamura, and Lynda D. Roman, "Racial and Ethnic Disparities in the Use of Robot-Assisted Surgery for Endometrial Cancer Management: A Population-Based Study," Cancer Epidemiology, Biomarkers & Prevention 33, no. 1 (2024): 20–27, https://aacrjournals.org/cebp/article-abstract/33/1/20/732007/Racial-and-Ethnic-Disparities-in-the-Use-of-Robot.
xcvi.	"About CRSA," Clinical Robotic Surgery Association, accessed December 24, 2024, https://clinicalrobotics.com/about/?utm_source=chatgpt.com.
xcvii.	Willie Underwood, Wei Wei, Stacey Rubin, Javier Hernandez, Xianglin L. Du, and Linda S. Volk, "Racial treatment trends in localized/regional prostate carcinoma: 1992–1999," Cancer 103, no. 3 (2005): 538–545, https://doi.org/10.1002/cncr.20796.
xcviii.	Michael Argenziano, Mehmet C. Oz, Timothy DeRose, Takushi Ashton, Craig R. Smith, Daniel Landau, and Aubrey C. Galloway, "Totally endoscopic atrial septal defect repair with robotic assistance," Heart Surgery Forum 5, no. 3 (2002): 294–300.
xcix.	Jens J. Stein and Nikhil Panda, "Robotic Surgery and Implications for Jehovah's Witnesses," in Caring for Patients Who Refuse Blood Transfusions: A Guide to Bloodless Medicine and Surgery, ed. Jean-François Hardy (Springer International Publishing, 2022), 179–186, https://doi.org/10.1007/978-3-030-92566-0_18.

www.ingramcontent.com/pod-product-compliance
Lightning Source LLC
Chambersburg PA
CBHW072155070526
44585CB00015B/1155